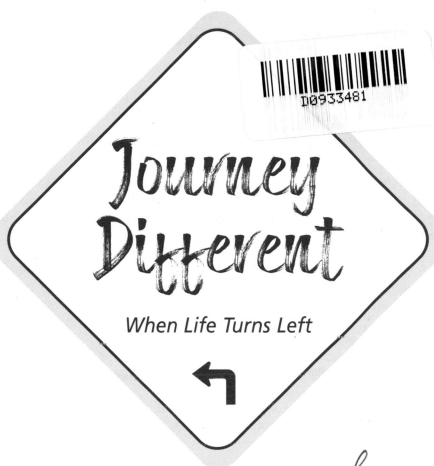

Journey Different

When Life Turns Left

Blessings on your Journey!

JUDY SWIFT

Judy Swift

ISBN: 978-1-943361-55-7
Ebook ISBN: 978-1-943361-56-4

Library of Congress Control Number: 2019931436

Printed in the United States of America

ENDORSEMENTS

I have known Judy Swift for forty-two years, lived with her, been mentored by her, and have a rich friendship with her. *She is my mother.* My mother is fiercely passionate in her love and worship of the Lord. You will see and gain in these pages what she pours out without inhibition. You will discover truth told in its rawest form. You will be moved by a heart that has weathered crushing storms, yet stood staunchly in love and trust for the Lord. More importantly, you will be inspired with a longing to know the indescribable God who reveals Himself undeniably and beautifully throughout her lifetime. I am confident that all of you who read this book will walk forward with a revelation of the goodness and realness of the Father and with a craving in the deepest part of your being to know Him even more.

> Jessica Rice
> Daughter of Judy Swift, Interior Designer
> Tulsa, OK

As most of us are fully aware, life is FULL of mountaintops, cliffs, and plateaus. And then there are, or course, the valleys. I have witnessed my mother, Judy Swift, stand tall on mountaintops, refuse to give up on the difficult and despairing cliff edges, stand still and wait on the Lord on the plateaus, and remain faithful and unwavering in the deep dark valleys. And through all of those places in life, she has remained strong with the same testimony, "God is faithful, He is good. And I will not give up." I have watched my mother NEVER, NEVER give up. I have watched her remain standing, even when it seemed like it was impossible to stand any longer. Her story impacts many, and I truly believe it will meet people in all the different mountaintops, valleys, cliffs, and plateaus that they walk through in life.

> Rebekah Sullivant
> Daughter of Judy Swift, Singer/Songwriter, Associate
> Director of Music
> Christ Presbyterian Church, Nashville, TN

When Judy talks, I lean in. The way that she carries the deep truths of the gospel and the exuberant joy of the Lord with such a beautiful balance of tension is nothing short of a miracle. Her storytelling draws me in; laughing, crying, rethinking, and reimagining truths and beliefs. I always come away challenged to go deeper with Jesus. Judy's vulnerability and honesty are refreshing and clear the air for transformation to take place. Thank you, Judy. Your words are a much-needed gift!

> Kaye Haun
> Former Women's Pastor
> Lighthouse Church, Frisco, TX

It is impossible to know Judy Swift and remain unchanged. She inspires righteousness, peace, and joy (the kind that comes from walking with God). All those near her get the benefit. Her laughter is contagious, her up-close love is unwavering, and her wisdom is something I can't imagine living without. Truly, one of my life's greatest privileges is to call Judy my friend.

> Pastor Ken Williams
> Director, Equipped to Love
> Bethel Church, Redding, CA

My wife, Connie, and I have walked alongside Steve and Judy as friends for over thirty-five years. We have been close witnesses to their happiness and joys of life. We have witnessed them walking through death and real hardship, but "joy comes in the morning." This book will bring hope, healing, and inspired life to many.

> David and Connie King
> Friends and Business Owners
> Van Buren, AR

I have known Judy Swift for over two decades and have watched her influence everyone around her. She is honest, transparent, wise, challenging, funny, and down-to-earth. Judy has birthed joy and walked through the fires of her faith being tested like no other. You will find her encouraging and inspirational as you read her story, and perhaps get the opportunity to sit down for a good cup of coffee and a long chat with her! A must-read!

> Pastor Lloyd Rindels
> New Day Church, Kansas City, MO

As someone who has walked through the deepest valleys on the darkest of days, Judy transparently and openly invites you into a glimpse of her world . . . but the unexpected thing is, you won't find it dark where she's taking you! Her actions, attitude, and her writing exude a life full of joy, comfort, peace, and hope—seemingly counterintuitive for someone who has suffered great losses and known the depths of pain. This isn't a book about coping, but truly living even when life doesn't go as planned.

> Rachel Wimpey
> Artist, Painter, Classmate, and Friend of Bethany
> Tulsa, OK

I have known Judy Swift for decades and her storytelling ability married to her deep connected relationship to God have made her an amazing inspirer. Through sharing from her own very vulnerable life process, she engages us with inspiration that will create in us hope and faith that will cause you and me to live out a very brave life.

> Shawn Bolz
> Author and Host
> Los Angeles, CA
> www.bolzministries.com

Judy Swift is an incredible communicator. She is an incredible person. Judy's life has been a great example and influence for so many. The way she shares herself is a true reflection of the Father's heart and love for His people.

> Senior Pastor David Bendett
> Rock City Church
> Corpus Christi, Texas

Twenty-two years ago, I was part of a move of God that impacted our local region in a powerful way. It was in this season that I met Steve and Judy Swift, and their daughters, Jessica, Rebckah, and Bethany. They opened their home and lives to me, and it was through them that I powerfully experienced the Father's heart of God that launched my calling to the Kansas City House of Prayer for eighteen years, and now, as a conference speaker worldwide. In our darkest hour, when our one-year-old son suddenly died, I don't know if we would have been able to make it without the presence of this family, their prayers, their words, and their love. The Swifts hold one of the dearest places in my heart.

> Corey Russell
> Upper Room Church
> Dallas, TX

Judy Swift has walked through heartaches in life that I pray none of us will ever go through. As you read her book, you will cry, you will laugh, you will rejoice in God's faithfulness. Her book will inspire you to choose life, even in your darkest hour. Judy has chosen victory over defeat, joy over despair, and hope over hopelessness. Judy Swift is a hope-filled, joy-filled, life-giving woman of God. I am blessed to call her friend.

> Associate Pastor Susan Moore
> Sojourn Church
> Dallas, TX

DEDICATION

To Steve, my husband and best friend. It was your strength in the beginning and my strength in the middle. But, in truth, it was in the beginning, middle, and forever the strength of God's love and His faithfulness that carried us through the experiences described in this book—from tragedy and trial into triumph. I claim with you the truth found in 1 Corinthians 13:13, "And now abide faith, hope, love, these three; but the greatest of these is love."

I am so thankful for God's love, our love, our marriage of more than forty-five years, and the lives of our fantastic daughters, who are now married with three children each of their own. I thank you all for supporting and encouraging me in this undertaking of writing this book, which has held me captive until I finished it and felt released.

The trials and triumphs in our lives certainly had their eternal way and purpose for each of us. We have been refined, made stronger in character, and have attained much more confidence in hearing God's voice and experiencing His presence.

To Rebekah and Jessica. I have heard your stories about the deaths of your brother, Andrew, and your sister Bethany, and witnessed many hearts' doors open, allowing you to share the testimony of Jesus in profound ways. You have not wasted your sorrow. I am so proud of you.

To Grace Ann, whom I never had the joy of knowing fully. I shall meet you face-to-face in heaven.

To Andrew, our beloved and only son. You absolutely delighted all of our hearts for eighteen months, and your tragedy broke open heaven's voice and grace in an everlasting way.

To Bethany Joy, our youngest daughter and "our joy, our joy." I am thankful that you know not only Andrew fully alive now, but also Grace Ann.

To Debbie Stuckey, my dear friend whose own writings and heart I cherish. Thank you for your gentle direction that pressed me to go from teaching to deeply sharing.

I also dedicate this to those who were with us in the hospitals, during our times of grieving, and all of the years before, during, and after. I love you more than words can express.

"We—or at least I—shall not be able to adore God on the highest occasions if we have learned no habit of doing so on the lowest. At best, our faith and reason will tell us that He is adorable, but we shall not have found Him so, not have 'tasted and seen.' Any patch of sunlight in a wood will show you something about the sun which you could never get from reading books on astronomy. These pure and spontaneous pleasures are 'patches of Godlight' in the woods of experience."

—C. S. Lewis

"Christ spoke, and all of heaven was in it."

—Judy Swift

CONTENTS

Foreword..11

Preface...13

  1. Seeing Life from Both Sides...15

  2. A Good Start...17

  3. The Love of My Life..23

  4. Godly Guide to Higher Paths...27

  5. Natural and Spiritual Growth..33

  6. Oh, What a Beautiful Morning!..41

  7. Every Word Spoken Has Power..49

  8. Family Forgiveness . . . and Then the Crash................57

  9. Saying Good-Bye..65

10. A Point of No Return...71

11. Becoming Official...75

12. The Wonder of Hearing God's Voice................................81

13. Two Challenges: Hearing, Then Agreeing.....................91

14. Step into the Quiet—Listen..97

15. Waiting Is Not a Bad Thing...105

16. Fine Wine Takes Time...115

17. My Joy! My Joy!...125

18. Growing Up . . . with Mom and Dad.............................133

19. The Call in the Night..139

20. Bethany's Memorial..145

21. Seeing with Spiritual Eyes...151

22. Choices with Sight and Sound..159

23. Be Mindful of Words Spoken...165

24. Learning to Trust *More*..169

25. Heart Connection..175

26. From Glory to Glory...185

Epilogue: And Now 189

Appendix A: Tributes to Andrew and Bethany...............191

Appendix B: Jessica and Rebekah Remember..................199

FOREWORD

When darkness comes and shadows our lives,
We lose our vision, and we can lose our way.
We need a voice to light our way,
To go forward; to not stumble; to not be lost.
　　　　　—Steve Swift, "Moving Out of Darkness"

Many years ago, as a graduate student, I heard a knock on the door of my apartment. I opened the door, and there she stood—a young woman with lightning flashing from her brown eyes and a smile that captured my heart in an instant! One week later, we both knew that we would be married. We had found the soul mate, the life friend, and the love of our lives. We were married, launched our careers, and had three daughters and a son. God had captured our lives, and we joyfully engaged our lives in serving Him.

In a most unexpected moment—at a high point of marriage, career, serving, friendships, and family life—tragedy invaded our home and darkness surrounded us.

This book is the chronicle of Judy's journey through the challenges and her triumph on the other side. She writes as a mom, a wife, and a real-life fighter finding her way through, not to be a survivor, but to be a victor.

Judy is an amazing wife, mother, friend, witness, and person. She is an interior designer, speaker, counselor, and, now, an author. She says that writing this book has been the most difficult thing she has done in her life. She had never wanted to be a writer, and telling her story required her to relive the moments, memories, and miseries of the darkest times of her life. Even through this struggle, writing this book has allowed her to proclaim triumph once again—the victory of overcoming challenges and living life fully. I am an eyewitness to her journey through the darkness and into the light.

Judy tells her story now to pronounce the goodness of God and his faithfulness to redeem even our greatest losses. She speaks at women's retreats, church gatherings, to the person next to her at a coffee shop, to the lady behind her in line at the movie theater, and to people who come to our home because they are struggling and cannot find their way. Opportunities to share empathy and compassion to those who are hurting and to those who are in dark seasons of their lives are all around her. She lives ready to share, encourage, and share hope from her own life.

I love Judy, and I am so proud of her. I am proud when I am in a room with her. I am proud when I watch her minister to a hurting friend. I am proud of her for writing this book. I am proud to have her by my side.

Writing this book has given Judy the opportunity to share her story of God's goodness with many more people—most importantly with *you* as you read this book. Read the words, but also listen to her heart. Her testimony of hearing God's voice guiding her through her darkest moments can become your testimony. Her victory can become your victory. Read . . . and listen. Hear God's voice showing you the way through your most difficult moments, or perhaps, helping you show a friend through their darkest times.

> *Your ears will hear a word behind you,*
> *"This is the way, walk in it"*
> (Isaiah 30:21 NASB).

PREFACE

While ordinary or grand experiences in this world have brought me amazement, satisfaction, and profit; it is in the *extraordinary* experiences, these patches of light that I have encountered from another world, that have profited my spirit, my thinking, and my life by a truly supernatural God who makes Himself known on earth today.

C. S. Lewis wrote: *"If you read history you will find that the Christians who did most for the present world were those who thought most of the next. The apostles themselves, who set out on foot to convert the Roman Empire, the great men who built up the Middle Ages, the English evangelicals who abolished the slave trade, all left their mark on earth, precisely because their minds were occupied with Heaven. It is since Christians have largely ceased to think of the other world that they have become so ineffective in this one. Aim at Heaven and you will get earth 'thrown in.' Aim at earth and you will get neither."*

When I counsel or teach, I am often met head-on with a mind-set of limited or boxed-in thinking. I find that the power of thought keeps one "boxed in" to earth's perspective and/or religious thinking. The Bible tells us as a man thinks, so is he. It is time for us to change and lift our thinking higher. Once, when I heard the Lord's voice, He told me, "My ways are higher." I agree with C. S. Lewis, and I am going to aim for heaven!

This book is my story. It is true down to the last sentence. It is told from my perspective—the way I remember, the way I saw, and the way I heard. It is real, it is raw, and it is relevant for today's living. This book is my testimony. Every person's testimony is different, in part, because every person's perspective and experience with life and with the Lord is different. No two testimonies are the same, just as no two snowflakes are the same. Although each snowflake has three components—dust, water, and air—each one is different. All true testimonies have three components as well—the Lord's presence, power, and sustaining grace. These three things are what enabled us to overcome our circumstances and forever shaped our perspective.

I am an artist and an interior designer. I learned early in my art training that all perspective drawings begin with a vantage point and then diminish or come together at a destination point. This book is written from the vantage point of Jesus, and of knowing Him as my personal Savior and my Lord. It is through Him that eventually all things will diminish into the glory of heaven.

My prayer is that the Lord will reveal Himself to you more personally as you read this book and that you will see that He is sufficient—even more than sufficient—for all you need. There is no sorrow or joy that is unimportant in His eyes. He will weep with you, comfort you, confront you, and then spin your greatest sorrows or failures into genuine joy. Let yourself wonder and embrace the mystical unfolding of His everlasting love. Aim for God's kingdom and bring it to earth!

1

Seeing Life from Both Sides

"I never imagined it would be like this . . ."

Of course, you didn't. Who can possibly imagine precisely how their future will be?

I sometimes think of life as being like a labyrinth. *Merriam-Webster's Collegiate Dictionary* defines a labyrinth as "a place constructed of or full of intricate passageways and blind alleys." Life, to me, feels exactly like that at times.

I cannot imagine maneuvering through life on earth without the master designer of life, the One who already knows the way through and is able to help me either see the blind alleys or lead me out of them.

To make our way through the good, bad, expected, unexpected, light, and dark, we must know the Way. Jesus said of Himself, "I am the Way," and I know this is true.

In my life of sixty-plus years, I feel as though I could sing at least the first two lines of the Joni Mitchell song, "Both Sides Now," and I have become especially captivated by the verse about clouds.

> *I cannot imagine maneuvering through life on earth without the master designer of life, the One who already knows the way through and is able to help me either see the blind alleys or lead me out of them.*

What we fail to understand is that neither clouds nor life are controlled by human beings. Clouds can be beautiful one day, with shades of pink, purple, and gold, and the next day be dark, gray, and rumbling. I think life presents itself the same way.

What makes colored clouds breathtaking? What makes ominous clouds stand out? Light! The sun reflecting off various atmospheric particles or breaking over the darkness in a brilliant, bright, thin line is what causes us to whisper, "Aah, a silver lining."

I love clouds and I love to paint clouds, but to do so, I have to look up. This book is all about a *willingness* to look up when it is dark, and you feel you can't find your way. Silver linings on top of clouds remind us that the sun is still shining, even when a storm is looming. I love silver linings—they remind me that the light brings a higher perspective, or certainly, another perspective. Perhaps you have lost perspective that God's light still shines, even in the darkest storms of life. He has something new or renewed, something grand—something that brings an "aah" to your lips and a light to your eyes. Now is the day to walk into it.

Words for Reflection

"'For I know the plans that I have for you,' declares the Lord, 'plans for welfare and not for calamity to give you a future and a hope'" (Jeremiah 29:11 NASB).

Ask the Lord to show you His plans for you as you read. God does have a plan and a purpose for your life. It is a good plan and when you discover it and begin to pursue it, you will be more excited and hopeful about your future than you ever thought possible!

"See, I am doing a new thing! Now it springs up; do you not perceive it? I am making a way in the wilderness and streams in the wasteland" (Isaiah 43:19 NIV).

Ask the Lord to reveal Himself to you or to speak to you. Begin to develop an awareness that God is with you, He knows you, and He really loves you.

"Therefore the Lord longs to be gracious to you, and therefore He waits on high to have compassion on you. For the Lord is a God of justice; how blessed are all those who long for Him" (Isaiah 30:18 NASB).

2

A Good Start

Not everybody has a good start in life—I recognize that and accept that those who don't have a great beginning may be a half step behind on the racetrack of life, but I also believe that poor beginnings *can* be overcome.

I am grateful that I had a good beginning. My early years were filled with the love of family, many friends, and a future that seemed endlessly good. That's not a bad foundation for faith, hope, and love, and if you are a parent or grandparent reading this, I strongly encourage you to make a good start possible for the children you dearly love.

I don't want to mislead you, however, since a good start will never be a perfect start. In fact, a good start can blind a person to the hardship and sorrow in the world, and leave a person unprepared to deal with either.

My father's last name was Oswalt, but everyone I knew called him Ozzie. He was a physician finishing his residency at a hospital in Houston when he met my mother who was training to be a nurse. My father informed her soon after meeting her that she would never work, but rather, be a wife and mother of the five children he predicted they would have. He said that even before the wedding.

They had a whirlwind romance; getting engaged, married, and taking a train to San Diego for their honeymoon all before Dad was inducted into the navy as a medical officer at the naval base in San Diego.

As it turned out, my parents did end up having five children. My older brothers watched over me and were among my caregivers (although this is a generous term). After Mother died when I was in my thirties, my oldest brother, Chuck, lovingly referred to himself as the patron of the family. I suppose he lived up to this title as he held our family together and always reached out on our birthdays and special occasions. In fact, Chuck was the one who gave me away to Steve at our wedding, although he barely made it home from Vietnam in time. My brother Chip was the one who checked up on me throughout high school and during college—he was a good overseer. Bill was closest to me in age, always game to my shenanigans and ready for fun. Sadly, he was killed in an airplane crash. My youngest brother, Barry, has become one of my dearest lifelong friends. All of my brothers are physicians, which speaks to the wonderful example and hero our dad was.

I grew up in Fort Stockton, a town in West Texas, a couple hours from Midland. The beauty of our part of the world is found in the mesas and sunsets, but the *gold* is found in the people.

In my opinion, my father was the leading physician in the town. It seemed like everybody knew him, and he knew everybody, which, of course, meant that everybody in town knew me and my brothers. There was no place to hide, but also no reason to want to.

My father and brothers were avid hunters, and I grew up being able to shoot a gun well, as long as the target was a fixed object, not an animal or bird. On my very first hunting trip with my dad, mom, and two older brothers, I waited my turn—the oldest always got to fire first if a buck was spotted, and since I was the third in line, I always had to wait. My mom stayed inside of the truck while the rest of us waited in the back. Fate having its way, when my turn to shoot finally came around, so did the biggest buck. I raised my gun, but then I froze. Images of *Bambi,* the first movie I ever saw, filled my head, and there was absolutely no way I could fire that gun. Instead, the butt of my gun hit the side of the pickup truck, and the buck disappeared. My father yanked me out of the back of the truck so fast I didn't have time to explain that really it was my mother's fault, because when I glanced back through the truck's rear window, she mouthed the word

> *The two biggest spiritual events of my childhood didn't happen in church.*
>
>

"Bambi." He informed me, "Your hunting days are over." And they were, but I wasn't sorry.

I didn't have any problem with fishing, however, and my dad wanted to guarantee that I would fish with him, so he bought me a rod and a pink reel with the word "Princess" printed on it. As far back as I can remember, he always referred to me as his "little princess." I enjoyed learning to fish because it was just my dad and me, and because I could sunbathe on the boat.

We were a church-going family, and I grew up hearing all of the Bible stories in Sunday school, and attending youth group as I entered my teens. The two biggest spiritual events of my childhood, however, didn't happen in church.

When I was a girl—maybe nine or ten years old—I prayed one evening, "God, I want you to show me tonight that you are real." That night, I had an extremely vivid dream that I was on a mountaintop, perhaps a mesa, with the wind blowing and storm clouds swirling. The wind was so strong it caused the skirt of my dress to billow around me.

Suddenly the clouds parted, and a great hand reached down toward me and picked me up. I can still close my eyes and see every detail of that experience—it is so vividly and thoroughly etched into my spirit and my memory.

As I awoke to the sound of my mother calling me, the dream came to an end, with the great hand reaching once again through the clouds and setting me down. I instantly exclaimed, "You *are* real!" I had absolutely no doubt about that, not that morning and not any day since. *It truly was my first divine encounter with the power and presence of God, and it set the stage for a life of desiring more of the Lord.*

When I was fifteen, my best friend's mother and sister were killed in an automobile accident. Sally and I were almost inseparable growing up. She spent half of her life at my house, and I spent the other half at her house. I don't remember why we weren't together on that Friday night, but we weren't, so some of my mother's friends found Sally at a picture show and brought her to my house. She arrived knowing nothing about what had happened. When she walked in, she said, "What are we doing here?" I walked her back to my bedroom, and although I felt unqualified to impart this heartbreaking news to my dearest friend, I told her as simply as I could that her mom and sister had been in a car wreck. Her mother was in a coma (she later died), and her little sister had been killed instantly. Sally went into hysteria.

I had no idea how to respond, but I prayed, "Lord, if you are really real, then help Sally." Immediately, I could feel a calming presence fill the room, and Sally went from wailing to absolute stillness. That was the first time I truly felt the presence of the Lord. I knew God was real after my dream years before, but that night I *felt* that God was real and that He could be *experienced.* That's when a longing in my heart began . . .

However, that experience of feeling the presence of God was still having trouble taking hold over my greater desire to have fun.

If any of us kids ever got into trouble, it seemed like it was usually me, or at least I was the one who got caught—I always seemed to be pushing the limits. One night, a small group of us climbed some trees in the city park, and from our vantage point above the main drag of town, we tossed water balloons onto passing cars. Not surprisingly, we were all arrested, taken to jail, and told that we could go home only if we agreed to tell our parents what had happened. It didn't really *matter* that nobody and no car had been harmed by the water balloons, the rules were the rules. Breaking the rules means the potential for harm, and therefore, rules are to be kept strictly and completely. My father grounded me for one month and stuck with it.

A love for adventure and having fun can either be an advantage or a disadvantage, depending on one's perspective, and my dad and I had different perspectives on that point. Shortly after my grounding was over, I was asked to babysit my two little brothers, with no pay of course, while my parents attended the baccalaureate service for my oldest brother.

I knew that I had been left in charge, but since my friends who stopped by the house told me that we would only be away from the house for a little while, I went with them. As you have likely anticipated, my parents returned home before I did. I was filled with remorse for getting caught, and once again, I was grounded.

When I was a senior in high school, I was told that my dad had lymphoma, a type of cancer, and I became undone. This was my daddy and he was a doctor—he couldn't have cancer. In my Pollyanna thinking, I always felt we had the perfect family and that nothing bad would last for long. Somehow, my dad could always fix anything or anybody, except himself.

When I was barely eighteen, I entered Texas Christian University (TCU). My family expected me to train to be a nurse, and that's what I expected of myself too. I quickly discovered that I didn't enjoy science classes or studying as much as a health-care degree required. Then I decided to look into elementary education but realized that I would probably end up teaching little kids—not that I don't like little kids, but that's a true and valuable calling, which I did not have. From there, I wandered into the art department and discovered that I had a calling for art, especially interior design. I had no problem throwing myself into the art and design world—I loved every aspect of the work and creativity, and that has been true all my life.

Dad's treatment at Baylor University Medical Center continued in Dallas during my freshman year. He usually came to see me at TCU before he went to an appointment at Baylor. I knew that my father had cancer, but it never occurred to me that he wouldn't recover. He did well most of that year, but then his condition took a downward turn the last two months of my freshman year.

After my last final exam, I drove to Dallas to be with my mom and dad. As I walked through the door of his hospital room, I was shocked to see how much he had deteriorated physically in just a week's time. Seeing me in a state of shock and hopelessness, he quickly asked me how my finals had gone and, of course, what kind of grades I had made that semester. I told him I had a 3.7 GPA. He smiled and said, "That's my girl!" *Those were the last words I heard my father speak to me.*

Daddy's best friend, Bert Kincaid, walked down the hospital hallway toward Daddy's room the following day just minutes after he died. We were standing in the hallway outside of the room, and when we told Bert the news, he said, "I know. I came to take him home." Bert was a rancher and pilot, and he had arranged for Dad's body to be prepared for transport in his private plane. Now that is a true friend.

Words for Reflection

"I have leaned upon You since I came into this world; I have relied on You since You took me safely from my mother's body. So I will ever praise you" (Psalm 71:6 Voice).

God has been working in and through your life for all of your life!

Can you remember when something extraordinary or supernatural took place in your life?

3

The Love of My Life

In college I casually dated several guys, but toward the end of my junior year, I began seriously dating a medical student introduced to me by my older brother, Chip, who was still at medical school in Galveston. I thought I was head over heels in love with him when Molly, my childhood friend and roommate, told me that she wanted me to meet a guy named Steve Swift who happened to be sharing an apartment with her boyfriend.

When Molly and I knocked on the door to their apartment the following weekend, Steve greeted us with a guitar strapped to his shoulder and a wonderful smile and welcome. I was immediately captivated and so was he. While Molly's date finished getting ready for the evening, Steve entertained Molly and me by singing and playing his guitar. He had a great voice and an unspeakable joy that I couldn't fully describe, and it felt like something I had been seeking since my dad's death two years before.

Steve was completing his second year of seminary, although he was not planning on returning the following year. He had made the decision prior to meeting me to enter Trinity University in San Antonio, Texas, to complete a master's program in hospital administration; however, I was unaware of all of this. I just knew that, for this brief time together, I was drawn to his joy but I was dating a medical student who planned to marry me.

The following weekend, Steve asked me out on a date. I was so enamored. I tried to put aside the fact that he was going to be a preacher, since I had always believed that I was going to marry a doctor, like my daddy. This hesitation, however, was temporary and would quickly pass. We played miniature golf, which I lost. When we went out for Italian food afterward, Steve wrote on one of the paper napkins, "Now that I have found you, my lifelong search has ended, and at last, I have arrived at a beginning." He slid the napkin across the table. I read what he had written, and I knew in an instant that he was the only man for me. The temporary gave way to the eternal, and I was captivated.

We got married during spring break my senior year, and after a brief honeymoon, we moved into a tiny garage apartment until my graduation. It was there that I burned my first attempt at fried chicken. I had never cooked in my life—we had someone who cooked for us in our family as I was growing up—so I truly didn't know what I didn't know about cooking. Steve took one look at that charred chicken, still raw on the inside, and together we heartily threw it out into the yard. Thank goodness I had the foresight to sign up for Meal Management as an elective course during my last semester at TCU.

After graduating, we packed up our few new pieces of furniture and our personal belongings and moved to San Antonio, where Steve began at Trinity University. He received the Dean's Scholarship—only one given each year—which had a stipulation that the recipient could not be employed and had to maintain a 4.0 GPA throughout the year. That left me as the sole breadwinner, which was terrifying.

I had found a job at a commercial and residential design firm downtown. I started at the firm as a rookie-degreed interior designer—emphasis on rookie—until I got a shot at the big time. I was assigned to assist one of the company's designers on a job in Florida. Our client had a brand-new condo on the twenty-sixth floor of one of the foremost complexes in Miami at the time. The designer I was assisting had a minor heart attack, which meant that this rookie designer was now in charge of the project, and I had to make the first presentation on the client's yacht. He liked our design ideas and he liked me, so he decided to purchase the entire twenty-sixth floor. Working with this client and an unlimited budget was a dream come true, and it ended up being an incredible experience.

When Steve's year of school was up, we left San Antonio and I didn't get to see the completion of my work on the condo until years later, when the owner contacted me to do the design for his world headquarters.

Steve's dream also came true when he was awarded one of the top residencies for hospital administration at Baylor University Medical Center in Dallas, where I was hired to join the Baylor Medical Design Department. I found myself back in the very corridors where I had last seen my daddy alive—what a mixture of emotions!

> *It's strange how God's time is always the right time.*

After his year of residency at Baylor, Steve took a position at the Mercy Medical Center in Fort Smith, Arkansas.

Arkansas? Really? I had never lived outside Texas, so I felt like a traitor. The words of an old ballad, "The Cowman's Lament," ran through my mind.

Even so, Steve and I loved adventure and we were head over heels in love with each other. We quickly made good friends and we were both growing in our respective career fields, and that upward trajectory continued in Fort Smith. Once in Arkansas, we quickly found our way to a wonderful church with a strong Bible-preaching pastor. I would never have expected it, but Arkansas was exactly where I needed to be at that time. It's strange how God's time is always the right time.

Words for Reflection

"The steps of a good man are ordered by the Lord, and He delights in his way. Though he fall, he shall not be utterly cast down; for the Lord upholds him with His hand" (Psalm 37:23–24).

God delights in the good paths that He has prepared for us to walk in. He not only leads us into what we shall do, but the relationships that He desires for us to have.

The Lord meets you where you stand today. He is aware of your past steps and forgives your missteps. He wants to lead you in your future steps.

Do you feel that God has truly directed your life, or do you attribute to someone else your paths taken?

Do you feel like, out of desperation or rebellion, you took your own paths which may not have turned out so well?

It is never too late to get on the right path. In my life, I have found that when I humble myself to the Lord, a floodgate of love, mercy, and forgiveness pours into my hurting soul. He helps me up, pats me on the back, and says, "Get back in the game of life because I'll go with you on this higher way."

4

Godly Guide to Higher Paths

Once Steve and I got to Fort Smith, we wasted no time in joining the First Baptist Church. I discerned from our first visit that the members of this church truly knew the Word of God and I sensed that I would be the beneficiary of not only their knowledge, but also their love and fellowship. Remember, Steve had two years in seminary. I wasn't worried about him; I was worried about me and my complete lack of biblical knowledge. Appearance was very important to me.

The first Sunday that we attended the church, I went to the women's Sunday school for my age group. When I walked into the classroom, I discovered that I was the only woman there who wasn't carrying a Bible! I couldn't get over how well the teacher and everyone in the class knew the Bible. My very fear was becoming a reality.

After class, I met Steve in the Sunday school assembly room. "Why did you let me walk in that room without a Bible? I was the only one in there without a Bible! I was humiliated!" He replied very matter-of-factly, "You would have been even more humiliated if you had walked in with a Bible and then hadn't been able to find a passage of Scripture they asked you to look up." He was right. I just love that man and his wisdom!

Although I went to church in West Texas with my family every Sunday that we were in

> *I always seemed to push the edge. That "edge" tended to draw me to people of extravagant commitment.*

town, I didn't grow up reading the Bible, much less understanding it. I suppose I never thought I had the time to read such a laborious book. I put all of my focus into being a fun-loving girl, who mostly cared about being popular and how I looked, and I always seemed to push the edge. That "edge" tended to draw me to people of extravagant commitment.

In attending our new Baptist church and Sunday school, I wanted to appear like I was biblically adept, and I wanted to be accepted. It was a great feat of pretending; however, it never seemed to evolve into a passion that would cause me to really read the Bible. I wasn't growing spiritually; all I was doing was trying to project the right image of a Christian that I thought the church expected.

Although I grew up Methodist, I also wanted to be a nun. Our maids would take me to a Catholic church sometimes and they always gave me a rosary for Christmas. There was something noble and extravagant to me about a nun's commitment. I also liked the statues and burning candles—the Catholic church had an awe that drew me in. There has always been something inside me that has been drawn to the inexplicable awe of God.

After that first experience at Sunday school, I bought a Bible and, of course, had my name engraved in the leather. For the first time ever, I also began to read it. Frankly, I found it hard to read and somewhat boring, so I also got involved in a Bible study course that was aimed at evangelism, called "Evangelism Explosion." Those of us in the course were challenged to memorize one hundred verses and to fully learn the "Plan of Salvation" to present to people we encountered during our door-to-door visitation and outreaches. I initially signed up for the course because it had limited spaces, was taught by our brilliant pastor, and was the popular thing to do at our church. I wanted to fit in, and this program was the fast-track way to do that, at least in my opinion.

As part of the curriculum, each student was asked to write out his or her personal testimony. I had one big problem—I didn't have a testimony. I couldn't even answer the basic questions that were part of the preparatory questionnaire. I was confident that I would go to heaven when I died, but I had no real authority to back that up.

One night, after the pastor's assistant, Ann Curtis, and I had gone on a visitation outreach, she asked me while we were in the car, "Judy, why don't you tell me your testimony?" I hemmed and hawed, and although Ann didn't say much in response, I knew she realized that I didn't have a testimony. I felt like I had been set up!

There was a part in the evangelism presentation where we simply asked the person we were visiting, "Have you come to a place in your spiritual life that you know for sure that if you died tonight you would go to heaven?"

We heard so many different answers! Some were very straightforward and informed, while others were more convoluted and misinformed according to Scripture. That particular night, my assigned portion of the presentation was to ask that question. Even though it feels so formal and not the way I like to talk, it's essentially the same question I use today, just slightly altered to feel more natural. When I asked the question that night, the person's answer was convoluted and confusing not only to us, but also to himself.

When he had finished answering, I simply replied, "All you have to do is transfer all your trust from yourself to Jesus Christ alone to save you."

> *I knew I believed in God. I had experienced two remarkable encounters with Him growing up; however, I had never made an eternal transaction with the Lord—my life for His life.*
>
>

No sooner had I spoken those words than I heard a voice speak into my right ear, "But you have never done this."

I was bewildered! What did I just hear? I was rattled by this "voice" that I had just heard so clearly. Stammering, I looked around to see if anyone else had heard it. Ann stepped in and finished the presentation.

I knew I believed in God. I had experienced two remarkable encounters with Him growing up; however, I had never made an eternal transaction with the Lord—my life for His life.

Undone, I went home, fell on the floor of my bedroom, and asked Jesus to come into my life as my Savior. I first felt a strong peace, and then there was joy—the kind of joy I felt the night I met Steve. I had always been happy when things in my life were going well, but I never had that constant sense of joy that Steve had. That night, something in me changed.

I had been dedicated to the Lord when I was a baby, but now I was fully grown, full of faith, and a follower of Christ. Jesus was baptized as an adult, and therefore, I felt I also needed to be baptized as an adult.

The next Sunday, I walked forward at the altar call given by the pastor, and although he didn't know what was going on, Steve followed me. All the way down the aisle, Steve kept whispering over my shoulder, "What are you doing, Judy? Why are we walking down this aisle?" What did he mean, "we"?

At the front of the sanctuary, the pastor asked me, "Judy, do you have something you want to share?" I responded, "Yes. This week I invited Jesus Christ to be my personal Savior and my Lord, and I want to make a public confession about it." Steve was shocked. He had thought he had married a good Christian girl. The pastor was equally surprised, but for the first time, I didn't care what others were thinking about me. I knew that what I was doing had moved me into a new relationship with God, and I felt a deep peace that I had never felt before. Shortly after this, I was baptized.

My desire for Scripture grew exponentially, and I had an increased anointing and ability to teach my Sunday school class of fifteen-year-old girls. There was a profound change inside of me, even though on the outside, nothing appeared to be different. The fact that I didn't care what others thought was a seed that began to take root and has borne miraculous fruit throughout my life.

I began to share my faith openly. I shared with my baby brother, Barry, and my mother, and both invited Jesus into their hearts. My mother died about five years later and I was extremely grateful that I knew with certainty that she was with the Lord. Sharing your faith with family members probably feels the most difficult because family members *really* know you, and then you show up in all your newfound righteousness—or so they think—and you suddenly feel inadequate. Once again, I decided that I wouldn't worry about what other people thought when I shared my experiences with the Lord.

> *It had never dawned on me to evaluate my life—my attitudes, my ideas, my opinions, my behavior, my desires—according to the Word of God.*

However, I recognized that I still had much to learn about how to *live out* the fullness of my salvation.

What I thought about other people was simply that people "were the way they were"—which wasn't true in reality but was certainly true in the reality of my mind-set. What I thought about myself was determined the same way: it had never dawned on me to evaluate my life—my attitudes, my ideas, my opinions, my behavior, my desires—according to the Word of God. I wouldn't have been able to tell you where to begin in adopting that mentality without the wisdom and love of older women, who live uprightly with amazing, steadfast faith.

A Time to Grow!

When a fetus is born, it is then referred to as a baby. I knew that spiritually I had been born again, which was the phrase Jesus used when talking to a man named Nicodemus (see John 3:3). Instinctively, I knew that I now needed a mother—or a community of mothers—to help me grow.

God in His wisdom and goodness put three women in my way (some babies are a handful and I was one of them—God knew I would need more than one spiritual mother!).

Judy Guest. Judy was my first Sunday school teacher after Steve and I moved to Fort Smith. She had a kind way of teaching, and she always based her lessons on the Word of God. The biggest thing that captivated me was her deep knowledge of the Word of God—she could refer to a particular verse on demand. I often found myself wondering how anyone could know that many verses. I wanted to be just like her, speaking God's wisdom and truth rather than my own thoughts and opinions.

Kaay Gean. Kaay was my go-to woman whenever I thought I couldn't take any more. She always seemed to be available. When I would arrive at her home in a flurry or a fury, with her gentle and quiet spirit, she would pour me a cup of coffee in one of her lovely "little bird" china cups, saucer included. We would then sit by her sunlit bay window and I would talk, cry, and then talk some more. She would let me pour out my heart about the challenges of marriage and childrearing, and then respond with a story from her life that gave me the courage to believe that I would make it. When I finished my harangue, in the most heavenly perspective she would give me advice that was never too long or involved. Kaay especially counseled me in matters related to Steve and our daughter, who was born soon after my spiritual born-again experience. As she shared her difficulties in being a wife and mother, her honesty encouraged me more than she will ever know. In fact, few people have ever given me as much courage and hope as Kaay. Mystically, she could turn an ordinary temporal day into something eternal . . . and do it instantly.

Thelma Bradford. I called Thelma whenever I needed advice or counsel that was direct and to the point. I was usually on some sort of a mission when

I went to her home, saying, "Just give it to me straight," and then asking things like, "How can I fix Steve?" Step by step, she would lead me into knowledge and wisdom. She would talk about my calling as a wife and mother—the ministry of love to my husband and children—and would remind me to put matters of the home first and ministry to church and others second. That was to be my highest calling and reward, to have a husband who would love and adore me and children who, when grown, would one day bless and thank me. Thelma would usually end our time by reminding me that Jesus in His darkest hour said to His Father, "Not my will, but your will be done." I would go away promising myself to be a better wife, feeling humble, yet very grateful for such a brave woman who was willing to take on the challenge of me.

These women and their husbands mentored Steve and me. We needed all of them and they were always available, even when it was inconvenient.

I remember one night when I felt Steve and I were at an impasse —a nice way of describing our situation—and we called Thelma and Calvin's home. They told us to come over, even though it was really late. As we were leaving, I asked, "How can we ever repay you?" They simply responded, "You can't. There will be a time you will do what we have done, and that will be our payment." And so that's what we have done.

Words for Reflection

"And I will ask the Father, and he will give you another advocate to help you and be with you forever—the Spirit of truth. The world cannot accept him, because it neither sees him nor knows him. But you know him, for he lives with you and will be in you" (John 14:16–17 NIV).

"Older women likewise are to be reverent . . . so that they may encourage the young women to love their husbands, to love their children" (Titus 2:3–4 NASB).

"Older men are to be temperate, dignified, sensible, sound in faith, in love, in perseverance" (Titus 2:2 NASB).

Who are the godly guides that God has set in your path? Name them, and thank God for their good impact on your life. Then think how you may "pay it forward."

5

Natural and Spiritual Growth

Steve and I were not only growing in our love, marriage, and spiritual lives, but also in our family!

Our beautiful, brown-eyed daughter, Jessica, was born a year after my salvation experience. A month after Jessica's birth, my brother Chuck's wife, Bootie (which was somehow a nickname for Martha Ann), came for a visit to help out with our baby.

There was a lot of time to sit and chat while I nursed, and then sit and chat again while I washed and folded baby diapers—yes, in the beginning, I was one of those natural mothers. Everything had to be inconvenient and hard, you know, like a pioneer!

One day while we were talking, Bootie told me about visiting a church where some of the people were singing in another language. "What? Another language?" I asked her in shock. She said they called it "tongues."

I had never heard of such a thing. It sounded very strange to me, and yet, I was drawn to learn more. I was beginning to apprehend that God was mystical and supernatural, but I was still skeptical. For some reason, I believed that my limited knowledge was going to put an infinitely good God into my tiny little box.

Bootie asked me if there was a church like this in Fort Smith. I wasn't sure what "like this" meant, but I remembered that a band played worship songs for the teenage Sunday school department where Steve and I taught. The leader of the band, who was somewhat of a hippie, had a bookstore across from the local Sonic Drive-In, so I suggested that we start there.

We walked into the bookstore, Simple Life, in search of a book that might describe the experience that Bootie told me about. We bought a book titled *The Other Side of the Coin*, and we read it to each other over the next twenty-four hours.

The next night I left Jessica, fed and sleepy, with Steve, and Bootie and I went to the Bible study at Simple Life. When we walked in, Bootie announced to the group, "We are here to have somebody lay hands on us and give us the gift of tongues." We were so innocent and so "by the book." Looking back, it was probably one of the strangest nights in that little group of believers—and in my life and Bootie's life, too!

Several people in the group went with Bootie into a private room and before I knew it, she emerged with great excitement, telling me that she had prayed in tongues. Wow! This was just what we were expecting. My turn was next, but before I went into the private room, I called home to find out how Jessica was doing. Steve informed me that she was screaming her head off since it was feeding time. I raced home in my brand-new station wagon (that's what most mothers drove back then) to nurse Jessica and then turned around and went back. A few of the people in the group laid hands on me and prayed and prayed and prayed . . . and nothing happened. I was frustrated and began questioning my faith. The people continued to pray quietly for me and finally I whispered, "Lord, you said this is a gift given to those of us who believe in Jesus, and I desire this gift, but if you never give this gift to me, I'm all right with that. I trust you." After that little prayer, I felt a tremendous peace and the most profound sense of God's sweet presence. Then, I began to hear in my mind the Greek word, "Abba." My first thought was, "Oh, really. I know that word—I learned it in Evangelism Explosion. It means 'Daddy.' *Someone* is trying to make a fool out of me." My pride stood steadfast and I remained silent until I decided in my mind and in my heart that I didn't care if those praying heard me say "Abba" and nothing more. So, I relinquished my pride and the fear that I would appear foolish, and I began repeating, "Abba . . . Abba . . . Abba." Seconds felt like minutes before I realized that a language I had never learned or heard was flowing out of my mouth.

Steve was the most cautious, and perhaps, even skeptical about the whole experience. He listened to our story but still didn't want anything to do with what happened at the Simple Life study. He retreated to the viewpoint he learned during his seminary training that the gift of tongues was no longer relevant or needed for today. It's hard to convince someone who uses rhetoric, even if you hold the trump card of personal experience. I knew that I had asked for and received this experience through my faith, just as I had asked Jesus by faith to save me and become my Lord.

A few months later, Steve drove baby Jessica and me to Fort Worth for a weeklong visit with my mother and her husband. On his solo drive back home to Fort Smith, something happened to him as he was crossing the Red River.

Steve called my mother's house and my mother yelled to me, "Judy, Steve is on the phone." Walking across the living room into the kitchen, I heard the Holy Spirit say to me, "Steve has received the gift of tongues." When I greeted him, Steve nearly shouted, "You'll never believe what happened to me!" I said, "You received the gift of tongues." He questioned, "How did you know?" I said, "The same One who gave you that gift, told me." Yay, God!

Still More Growth Ahead

We had our second daughter, Rebekah, whom we sometimes called Beka. She more than doubled our joy as parents—how blessed we felt! We had two darling little girls to love, adore, and enjoy.

And then I became pregnant for the third time—the growing of our family seemed amazingly easy.

I was about six months pregnant when Steve, the girls, and I went out to Red River, New Mexico, to join my four brothers and their families. We had gone to Red River yearly for a family vacation when I was a child, and now we were taking our children to the place we all loved.

I made sure that I was taking care of myself—I didn't go horseback riding and I didn't overexert myself. I mostly just went from cabin to cabin, sitting on the porch and visiting with my family members.

It was a great, relaxing vacation, and the girls loved the trip and bonding with their cousins from Texas. After we returned home, however, I realized I hadn't felt our baby move in a while. A couple of days after returning, I saw my obstetrician, and he decided to do an ultrasound. There was no heartbeat. The doctor informed me, "Judy, your baby is not living." I was shocked and devastated.

The obstetrician made me an appointment at the hospital to induce labor and our baby girl was delivered. The nurse asked me if I wanted to see her or hold her. Steve decided to hold her, but I said, "No, I will see her in heaven." We named our third little girl Grace Ann because of God's grace and my middle name, Ann. Steve arranged for her burial while I was still in the hospital.

Our two little girls had been so excited about having a new baby in the family! When I returned home from the hospital, we told them their little sister had been born in heaven, not on earth. We explained to them why we had named her Grace, and that "grace" means a wonderful work of God, which their little sister certainly was.

Grace that Surpassed Understanding

In the aftermath of Grace Ann's death, we truly experienced moments of extreme grace, as well as hard work and great fun in our family.

Most of our life during those early days of parenting was very routine. We ate well, slept well, and played well. After a while, Steve and I got into flipping houses. With my design skills and Steve's growing skills as a carpenter, we found it fun—even exciting—to buy a great little house, live in it while we worked on it late at night and on weekends, and then sell it for a profit. Of course, our two daughters, six-year-old Jessica and three-year-old Rebekah, "worked" with us.

Jessica was a good little worker, and she also was very spiritually sensitive. When she was just four years old, she began to talk a lot about Jesus. She wanted to hear all about Him, and she truly wanted to *know* Him. I invited our music minister, Charles, over to the house one afternoon to visit with Jessica about salvation. She had a "crush" on Charles, and always wanted us to take her to greet him after church services. I thought he would be a safe and trusted friend who would discern the reality of this experience of salvation.

Frankly, a four-year-old's salvation was a strange concept to me—how could anyone that young understand God's salvation plan? Remember, I had been formally trained in Evangelism Explosion and was twenty-six years old when I invited Jesus into my life. *How could something so theological become so simple that even a young child could understand it?*

Charles was honored by the invitation, and he prayed with Jessica to invite Jesus to come into her life. The door to His kingdom was thrown wide open and our little girl walked through it—her love for the Lord became a demonstrative reality, and it continues to this day.

On the other hand, Rebekah was not as helpful of a worker—she was our singer and dreamer. One day, she would be Dolly, from *Hello, Dolly!*, donning one of my straw work hats and singing the entire soundtrack of the movie to Jessica while Jessica worked. The next day she might be Little Orphan Annie with her new tap shoes, and the next day she might be Laura Ingalls Wilder from *Little House on the Prairie*. Her world was never boring, and she kept Jessica well entertained (and sometimes frustrated).

Rebekah's love and gifting for music was evident at a very early age, so we gave her piano lessons. She excelled at playing piano, and quickly surpassed Jessica. She also exhibited a great gift to write songs—especially worship songs—early on.

Due to their gifts, the passionate lover of Jesus (Jessica) and the musical worshiper (Rebekah) were not only sisters who were close in age, but they also became best friends and remain close to this day, which makes me so happy!

One beautiful Saturday morning, Steve and I were working in the yard. After having breakfast on the patio, Rebekah, then three years old, drove her little red truck next door to visit with our elderly neighbors Bee and Bud. Bud liked to tinker in his garage and Rebekah would go to "assist him." We knew she was safe over there, and Jessica seemed happy to be "writing" letters to someone. Steve and I were getting a lot done in the yard—weeding and pruning trees and shrubs—and before we knew it, it was lunchtime.

After lunch, we put Rebekah down for a nap and Jessica continued to work on her mysterious little notes, while Steve and I went back to work. Jessica climbed high into one of the trees and was sticking her notes to different branches—she explained to us that she had written notes to Jesus and she wanted them to be easy for Him to find.

Thud!

All of a sudden, I heard a horrible sound. When I turned around, I saw Jessica lying facedown on the ground. She was dazed when I reached her. Turning her over gently, I was shocked and terrified when I saw her little arm. Her hand was bent backwards, both wrist bones were sticking out, and her elbow was dislocated. I gently laid her mangled arm across her chest, picked her up, and screamed for Steve. He came running and when he saw Jessica, he went straight into the house to call the emergency room and then ran upstairs to get Rebekah. We all made our way to the hospital, praying for an excellent orthopedic doctor to be on call and for the mercy and grace of God to pour out over each of us, especially Jessica.

> *This was the first major healing miracle we experienced in our family, and it also was the first time I felt the spiritual power that comes from declaring faith to combat fear. Fear is the enemy to faith. Fear traps us in early reality, while faith moves us to the impossible reality.*

After a five-hour surgery, the complex compound fracture was repaired by the very surgeon we had prayed for. Jessica was moved to a private room, where we learned from the doctor about the severity of the break. Dirt had gotten into her bones, so antibiotics were given with the hope that infection would not develop, but if it did, amputation was inevitable. The other big concern was that the break had occurred in her growth plate, so her arm might be stunted in growth.

Late that evening, after Steve left the hospital to go home with Rebekah, fear came into my heart like a flood. I spent the entire night by Jessica's bed, rebuking fear and speaking faith.

The following morning, the surgeon, with a resident by his side, stopped outside of Jessica's room before he came in to talk to us. I could hear him in the hallway describing the medical particulars to the resident. He ended by saying, "This is the worst compound fracture I have ever seen." Fear reared its ugly head again. We were told that Jessica would remain in the hospital for at least six weeks and would only be released if there was no sign of infection.

We called our friends and our church to ask them to pray for healing. Two weeks later, Jessica was released from the hospital with no infection, and her bones were healing without any sign of permanent injury to her growth plate.

This was the first major healing miracle we experienced in our family, and it also was the first time I felt the spiritual power that comes from declaring faith to combat fear. Fear is the enemy to faith. Fear traps us in early reality, while faith moves us to the impossible reality.

God values our faith, which is the place for us to surrender all of our self-effort. Through surrendering, we are able to truly adopt a position of absolute trust in our supernatural God who loves us and is for us. Trust makes us powerful and disempowers our enemy and his seeds of doubt, fear, and helplessness.

Words for Reflection

Jesus said, "For God so loved the world, that He gave His only begotten Son, that whoever believes in Him should not perish, but have eternal life" (John 3:16 NASB).

Belief (trusting in God) begins when you accept that He gave His Son as a sacrifice for all of your sins and shortcomings.

This "leap of faith" doesn't seem so big or difficult for a child; perhaps that is one of the reasons Jesus said to let the little children come to Him.

Salvation is a miracle. My desire is that it is only the beginning for many more miracles to follow us through life.

6

Oh, What a Beautiful Morning!

As delighted as Steve and I were with our family and life, there was one thing that Steve still desired: the birth of a son. He loved and adored his beautiful daughters, and to this day, he talks to them more than I do! However, Steve wanted a son, as I think many men do.

With the death of Grace Ann, and I in my mid-thirties, having another baby seemed impractical and problematic to me. I was looking at the situation totally from *my* perspective, not fully asking God what He wanted, but then one morning, I woke up with a desire to have another baby! On April 6, 1985, just after midnight, Stephen Andrew Swift was born, weighing in at eight pounds and six ounces. We felt so blessed with our strong, healthy son!

Our family had just moved into a new house that we had designed and built. Our new baby boy—we called him Andrew—had his own room, with every wall painted by me with a pastoral scene of sheep grazing on hills. I had painted a little white church nestled in the countryside, with "My sheep hear My voice, and I know them, and they follow Me" written in large cursive lettering circling the room (John 10:27).

One weekend, when Steve was on a solo campout, the Lord gave him a song. I couldn't tell you how many times I heard him rocking Andrew while singing his song.

My little lambs can hear Me,
They know My voice.
They show Me that they love Me,
And make My way their choice.

They follow Me through pastures green,
By waters cool and still.
They follow Me through valleys,
And over rocky hills.

Little Lamb, follow Me.
I'll love you as My own.
Little Lamb, follow Me,
I'll lead you safely home.
                    —Steve Swift, "Andrew's Song"

The girls loved their new baby brother—he ruled the house with his charming ways. Life for all of us couldn't have been happier or more complete!

Our home was situated on two-and-a-half acres with a large pond out front. We planted a willow tree, and a pair of mallard ducks found a new home there. The following spring, they had ducklings, and Andrew spent his days waddling around chasing the ducklings. Life was grand!

The following year we built a swimming pool, complete with a berm of landscaping—ornamental trees, shrubs, and an abundance of flowers. At my insistence, there was to be no fence to limit the view.

We had tremendous fun swimming as a family all summer, with friends and their children frequently visiting. The pool was a perfect addition to our property. We planned to close the pool in September, and keep it covered during the fall and winter. We were already talking about the additions we would add to it next summer.

It was a gorgeous Thursday morning in September—summer was lingering but fall was already starting to reveal its soon-to-be-brilliant colors. I had enjoyed a quick breakfast with Steve and our three children before Steve left for work and the three children left with their favorite babysitter, Julie, for several hours of fun. I had to throw myself into last-minute preparations for a bridal brunch I was giving for my friend's daughter, a young woman I had taught in Sunday school when she was a teenager.

I cut the last of the crape myrtle's fuchsia blooms, along with some deep-green ivy, and spun the two into a centerpiece for the main table. My heart was singing with joy as I picked up toys that were scattered around the pool in the backyard. I felt like nothing could spoil such a happy, beautiful day!

> *I was gaining the wisdom of capturing those small moments of love and fun, which are so fleeting.*
>
>

The brunch was a delightful success, and no sooner had the guests departed than Julie returned with the children from an adventurous outing. They had gone to a shoe store to try on the most ridiculous shoes they could find. By all accounts, Andrew had stolen the show when he paraded about the store in his T-shirt, diaper, and a pair of red high heels!

After the children came home, the girls ran outside to play. Andrew needed a nap and I needed to clean up, but first, I had a few moments to sit with Andrew in the hanging swing outside the back door of our kitchen. I was gaining the wisdom of capturing those small moments of love and fun, which are so fleeting.

Such moments, in many ways, are moments of eternity because they create joyful memories that can never be erased, even if the time is brief and the interludes are small. Schedules, plans, and busyness must give way to precious moments of expressing love—holding, kissing, and singing. Andrew finally fell asleep, so I laid him down and got "crazy busy" with hand-washing china, crystal, and silverware that had been used for the brunch. I didn't have much time until the little busybody would be up and about.

When Andrew was finished napping, he was excited about having a little snack and then playing with his new buddies on the back portico—a kitten that he carried in one arm and a puppy nipping by his side.

I checked on him several times and reminded Jessica and Rebekah to help keep an eye on him. I made myself a cup of coffee and sat down to look over the new textbooks that had arrived that afternoon. This was going to be my first year of homeschooling the girls, with an eighteen-month-old to boot!

All seemed happy and well.

The peace was shattered violently as Rebekah burst through the screened back door screaming, "Andrew! It's Andrew! Mother, he has fallen into the pool! We found him floating facedown!"

I bounded from my chair and when I reached the pool, Jessica was drenched, lifting Andrew's little body from the water and holding it up to me. He lay limp and blue in my arms—the same arms that had held him alive and with tenderness just a couple of hours before. My mind was racing. "Dear God—no, no! This can't be happening!"

My mind swirled with dozens of conflicting, bombarding thoughts, but all of the rest of the scene seemed to have stopped. It was surreal. Suddenly, as if slapped back into reality, I flew into action to expel water from his lungs and stomach as best I could, and I began mouth-to-mouth resuscitation. *What more should I do? I need help! It's no use! Don't give up! Fight, fight!* Nothing was working! I screamed, "Jessica, call 911."

Jessica ran into the house to call for an ambulance and I yelled for her to call her father and then our neighbor, too. Suddenly, I couldn't wait any longer—I could get to the hospital quicker than the ambulance would get to us.

I got in the car with my son in my arms, praying and doing everything I knew to do and calling upon the name of the Lord. As I neared the main road, I saw the ambulance that Jessica had called for. I began honking my horn and flashing my lights, but it drove past us. I pulled off the road, threw open the door, and began to run down the highway with Andrew in my arms. The ambulance driver caught sight of me in his rearview mirror and stopped. The other paramedic jumped out and ran toward me, took Andrew, and then we climbed into the back of the ambulance. I continued to pray and call upon the Lord Jesus as the paramedic sprang into action. There was still no sign of life.

Jessica called Steve. When he answered the phone in his office, he heard our two daughters screaming, "Daddy, Daddy! Andrew fell into the swimming pool and drowned. Mommy took him to the hospital!"

A lightning bolt of tragedy had burst out of a clear, blue sky and struck our eighteen-month-old son and our entire family.

As Steve raced to the hospital, he was pleading for Andrew's life. Andrew was his only son, his "son of promise." Up until that moment, Steve had seen himself as a happy, successful, young, Christian, American businessman, and the father of three wonderful children. His entire identity was shaken to its core.

Steve battled for Andrew's life in prayer, struggling against speculation but fighting to remain strong for me, Jessica, and Rebekah.

The emergency room staff had been alerted by the time we arrived: Code Blue! As they lifted Andrew from the ambulance and rushed him away from me, so many memories, fears, and what-ifs flooded into my mind. I felt utterly overcome and alone. Words seemed to crash down on me—some of hopelessness and some of strength. "We can make it through this. Steve and I and God . . . we can do it!" Then all of the swirling thoughts and emotions seemed to stop. I felt as if I was floating on a sea of nothingness, in a total daze.

A nurse kindly escorted me inside to wait in a nearby examination room. I was alone, even though various staff members offered words of comfort. I could feel my inner soul slipping into a depth of despair. Nothing that anybody said could reach me, and to be perfectly honest, I didn't want to be consoled. I didn't want to be there! I didn't want to be feeling or thinking or experiencing what I was facing. I wanted to die . . . and yet, if there was any chance that my son might live, I wanted to live. I felt such extreme conflict!

All of a sudden, a dear Christian friend, the first to arrive, walked through the emergency room door, bringing hope and faith with him. He didn't have to say a word. I knew we were agreeing for the same thing—Andrew's life. A short time later, Steve arrived—as much as I had wanted to die a few minutes earlier, I certainly didn't want to leave Steve and our daughters. A glimmer of light began shining over the darkness of my despair, and that light grew larger and brighter as other Christians, friends, neighbors, acquaintances, and even people in the hospital I had never met, began to gather around with such compassion.

At one point, I got up and wandered back into the area where the hospital staff was trying to revive Andrew. I felt as if I was in limbo, suspended between two very real worlds—life and death. The medical staff did their work very professionally and methodically. Some seemed to register fleeting moments of hope, but for the most part, there was no hope in the room. Even so, I knew that the emergency room doctor was a Christian, a believer in Jesus, so I knew he would not give up easily.

Andrew began to show some vital signs of life. A real sense of joy, hope, and victory exploded in the emergency room! Andrew was moved to a private, pediatric intensive care unit, and those of us in the waiting area moved, too. There was much more watching, waiting, and praying to be done.

In Andrew's private ICU room, there was so much commotion. People were scurrying—both doctors and nurses—as machines were hooked up to his body, an intravenous drip was started, and various acquaintances and friends of ours began arriving and gathering in the hallway outside his room. It all still felt very surreal to me.

What had started as a lovely Thursday morning turned into a dark and turbulent night. As exhausted as I was, I didn't want to sleep. I was awake and I was desperate for Andrew to wake up! I stifled the impulse to shout, "Wake up! Wake up and let me see your little brown eyes and hear your sweet voice!" His body was still, unresponsive, and hooked up to the machines that were doing the work of living for him. He *looked* peaceful . . . but I learned that night that *the appearance of peace can have an eternal perspective as well.*

A neighbor brought our daughters to the hospital. When Jessica walked into the room and saw him for the first time since he had left our home, the first words out of her mouth were, "Mother, Andrew has seen Jesus. He doesn't want to come back home."

I could hardly believe what she was saying. I responded, "Jessica, don't say that! We want him to come back." Jessica didn't reply to me, but later she told me that she had sensed the very real presence of Jesus when she entered Andrew's room. *The reality of the Lord's love and grace in that room had been revealed to her, a ten-year-old, but not to any adult.*

A business acquaintance visiting Steve in the hospital said, "I love children, but I don't know what it is about Andrew. I am so drawn to him." Later, we were told by a number of the nurses who cared for Andrew that they had talked among themselves, saying, "What is it that is so different when we walk into Andrew's room?" They said they could feel a difference. They had no answers as to why, and neither did I. I knew the love I felt for my son, but it didn't really enter my consciousness that other people were feeling the love of God.

At about nine o'clock that night, five or six hours after we had first lifted Andrew from the pool, the girls went to a friend's home to spend the night.

For a brief moment, I was alone. I wanted to be alone with my son, just the two of us together. I had spent much of the time earlier that evening standing outside the door to his room, content to watch him from a distance—there was not enough space for me in the room with the pediatrician, two nurses, and others who were constantly checking on him.

As I stood there at his door, I watched him as he slept. I longed to hold him, talk to him, touch him. I resented others touching him—at times I wanted to scream, "Leave him alone! You've messed with him enough. Just leave us alone. He's tired and I'm tired."

I grew exhausted of waiting. There is a special weariness that comes with hours of waiting for something—anything—to happen, only to have nothing happen.

Then something did happen. God spoke to me in my spirit, like He had done before on that night while I was presenting the gospel. *"Waiting is not a bad thing,"* He said, loudly enough that I could clearly hear it over the soft commotion within the room.

Words for Reflection

"But seek first the kingdom of God and His righteousness, and all these things shall be added to you. Therefore, do not worry about tomorrow, for tomorrow will worry about its own things. Sufficient for the day is its own trouble" (Matthew 6:33–34).

> *We must never live in either yesterday or tomorrow. We are only given grace to live in this day!*

"God is our refuge and strength, a very present help in trouble" (Psalm 46:1 NASB).

In John 14, the Lord says that His Spirit will be in you and will never leave you or forsake you.

> *In your deepest depths of despair in life, know this:*
> *God is not judging you or leaving you alone.*
> *Let the Father love you and guide you.*
> *Let Jesus redeem your trial.*
> *Ask the Holy Spirit to guide and comfort you.*

7

Every Word Spoken Has Power

With His words . . . swoosh, there was peace. A supernatural rush of God's presence washed over me and through me. A peace and presence filled Andrew's room and overflowed out into the hallway.

I thought in my spirit, *"I can do this. I can wait. I can wait on God, and I can wait on Andrew."* A supernatural calmness descended, and I knew that it had absolutely nothing to do with my ability or willpower. It was a gift from God.

It was only then, for the first time since coming to the hospital, that I became aware of the other people around me. I also became aware of my own body and clothes. I was still wearing the dress I had on when I had desperately expelled water from Andrew's lungs and stomach. I smelled terrible! A nurse gave me some scrubs, so I went and changed clothes and freshened up. Then I went to sit on the floor outside of Andrew's room with some friends. We laughed through tears, told happy stories about Andrew, and spoke words of hope to one another.

The nurses had allowed the doctors' dining room, next to the pediatric ICU, to be available for the overflow of people standing in the hallway after visiting hours.

Steve and two of his close friends who had come to the hospital were praying in a small room located down the hall from Andrew's room. They focused their prayers on a deep appeal to the heavenly Father to relent and allow Andrew to come back to "our home." In some ways, it reminded me of little boys who would beg a parent, "Please let him stay and play a little longer."

When the lead pediatrician entered that little prayer room to give an update to Steve, the presence of God came so powerfully upon the doctor that he fell to his knees and began confessing his sins and repenting before the Lord. Later, he told us that he had seen the Lord "high and lifted up" in that little room. A deep and lifelong change began in this physician's life that night. *Again I was reminded that waiting, particularly when waiting on the Lord, is not a bad thing.*

Andrew made it through the long and dark night. I remember it was very early in the morning that the Lord spoke clearly to me for a second time. All of the city and most of the hospital seemed to be asleep, but I was awake and feeling restless again. The peace that had sustained me through the night began to ebb and flow with fear and desperation once more. I had waited patiently, but enough was enough! I was losing sight of "eternity time" as I whispered to God, "Come on, Jesus! What is taking so long?"

It was as if a deluge of dark despair began to overwhelm me just before I heard the Lord's words, ***"Your water shall be turned to wine."*** The flood of despair came to a screeching halt as peace and stillness began to take hold once again. I felt His presence surrounding me. In a moment of hearing God's voice, despair and anger gave way to hope.

My water would be turned to wine? What could that mean? I had heard the Lord's voice so clearly, but I was still left wondering, "What is He saying? It doesn't make sense."

After checking all of the monitors that morning, the pediatrician said to me, "All systems are go. We are just waiting for little Andrew to wake up." After he left, I recalled that turning water into wine had been Jesus' first public miracle. I claimed that for Andrew. God was going to raise up Andrew and it would be the first of many miracles for our son!

My mind was racing out of control and seeking to take charge. I thought that if I willed it hard enough, whatever I wanted would come to pass.

But what had happened to waiting and trusting?

I had stepped back into an active exertion of my will. I had obeyed the Lord and I had waited long enough! I took back the control—I had to do something. Anything was better than nothing, or so I thought.

When I look back, I knew then and I know now in my heart that this rationale was not true. I had walked with God long enough to know that God does not communicate with me through thoughts of the mind—He communicates with me in my spirit.

My two older brothers came from Texas at different times to be with us in the hospital. They observed and mingled with friends and acquaintances. Although they were both physicians, we didn't discuss Andrew's medical details—it was enough for me that they were there with me.

Friday turned into Saturday, and Saturday turned into Sunday, but there were still no changes. There was no miracle. On Sunday as we were driving my brother, Dr. Chip Oswalt, to the airport, he tried to talk to me from his experience as a cardiovascular surgeon. He asked me what I thought was a reasonable amount of time to leave Andrew on life support if there were no significant changes. I became enraged. I told him that this was not a concern for me because God was going to raise Andrew up. I felt both volatile and vulnerable at the same time.

As we continued to the airport, Steve told me that since early that morning, he kept hearing in his spirit, *"Though you slay me, yet will I hope in you."* "What? Where did that come from?" I defiantly asked him. The passage came out of the book of Job. I had never read Job—I had never wanted to. And now God was speaking to us through the very book I always skipped because I thought it was filled with too much suffering.

I responded with adamant rejection of his words—I was furious! "Steve, that verse, that word, or whatever you want to call it, is not for us—not for me!" Chip had remained quiet during most of our conversation, but then he said, "Judy, you might want to listen to what Steve is saying."

I was terrified that the word might be true, and I was also terrified that it might mean Steve was giving up. I refused to even consider that God's word to me about "turning water into wine" could mean something besides a miracle. Was God going to bring Andrew from life on this earth into a glorious life with Him in eternity? No, no, no. This was not what I wanted.

I had concluded that Andrew was improving—that he was responding to the sound of our voices. It was what I wanted to believe. It was what I imagined was happening. I was already starting to make plans for when we could take Andrew home and give him his first bath, cleaning his dirty little

> *"I have learned three things about God: One, you cannot control Him. Two, you cannot obligate Him. Three, you cannot manipulate Him. He is God. If God never does another thing for you, He has already done too much by sending His only Son to die on the cross for you."*
>
>

fingernails from his last playtime outside. Didn't Steve listen to the doctor when he said we were just waiting for Andrew to wake up? No—I refused to listen to anything that was said to me that I didn't want to hear!

On Monday morning, I made the familiar trek down the hospital corridor to Andrew's room, secretly pleased with myself that I was staying strong in my faith. I had done all I knew to do. I was just waiting for God to do His part and wake Andrew up.

After checking on Andrew, I went to the small office that the hospital administration had graciously given us for privacy. Steve and his three faithful friends were there. They truly were a constant—there at the end of every night, there again at five thirty in the morning when Steve arrived. I sat down at the table with these men, and with resolve, I said, "If God does not raise up Andrew, I will never serve Him again. Oh, I will love Him, but I will not serve Him."

The room grew deathly quiet.

One of the men said, "Oh, Judy, you don't mean that. You're just not thinking straight right now."

I said firmly, "Yes, I mean that."

Compassionately, but strongly, the other said, "Judy, you have an evil and wicked heart and you need to repent." Steve remained seated by my side, but ever so quiet.

When I heard those words, I exploded with, "Explain yourself!"

He said calmly, "I have learned three things about God: One, you cannot control Him. Two, you cannot obligate Him. Three, you cannot manipulate Him. He is God. If God never does another thing for you, He has already done too much by sending His only Son to die on the cross for you." He concluded, "Judy, you need to repent. Change your thinking and change your speaking. He's God, Judy. He is God."

Truth broke through the barrier of delusion I had so carefully constructed during the previous three days. The defensive wall of pride I had built was shattered. Brokenness washed over me like a waterfall. I was spiraling down quickly, and I needed help! I needed God's help. I felt no condemnation from God—only His great love and forgiveness. I knew deep within that God would help me. He would see me through.

I threw my head onto my arms on the table and began to bawl my eyes out. As I cried and cried, various images came flooding into my memory.

I saw Andrew going to our refrigerator, opening it, and pulling out one of the little hospital nursery bottles that I had brought home after he was born. I kept them filled with milk in the refrigerator door for Andrew to drink as he desired. There was no schedule with our third child! I saw him running through the house with that little bottle dangling from his sweet, red lips. I said to the Lord, "*I give him up to you, Lord.*"

Then I saw Andrew sitting in his crib with his chubby little legs sticking through the slats on the side of the crib, smiling cheerfully at me when I would come in to pick him up in the morning. I said to the Lord, "*I give him up to you, Lord.*"

I saw Andrew opening his own cup of yogurt and then painting the kitchen wall with some of it. I said to the Lord, "*I give him up to you, Lord.*"

I saw Andrew playing with his little, wooden shoe bench, diligently beating each peg through its hole with a small, wooden mallet. "*I give him up to you, Lord.*"

I saw Andrew laughing and spraying our mallard ducklings with the garden hose. "*I give this joy to you, Lord.*"

> *In that hour, God's forgiveness freed me from self-sufficiency and self-strength. His love and mercy restored me.*
>
>

I saw Andrew sitting so contented in his daddy's lap on the lawn tractor as they mowed two acres of grass together. "*I give him up to be seated with you.*"

I saw Andrew's sweet smile with the funny little space between his front teeth. "*I give him up to you, Lord, for your pleasure.*"

As memory after memory came to my mind, I gave them all to the Lord. I yielded and entrusted my son to our heavenly Father.

When the memories subsided, I stopped crying. I had fully repented for the harsh thing I said about the Lord.

In that hour, God's forgiveness freed me from self-sufficiency and self-strength. His love and mercy restored me. At last, I surrendered to His will and I said, *"Not my will, Lord, but your will be done."*

> **He had been the voice of severe mercy to me, and in that, there is love. Speaking truth requires the sacrifice of self-preservation.**
>
>

The word that God had spoken to Steve, "Though you slay me, yet will I hope in you," no longer seemed so harsh, so unbearable, so insurmountable.

I gave my son back to God—my only son, the son who was supposed to carry on the Swift name, the son we had longed for and dearly loved every single minute that he was with us. Together, Steve and I confessed, "Lord, whether Andrew lives or dies, we will love you, serve you, and hope in you for all of our lives."

As I wept before the Lord, the men in the room wept with me. All of heaven must have been crying, as grace and mercy were poured into me.

When I finished talking to the Lord, the friend who had spoken to me about my need to repent said, "I wonder how many light-years we've traveled? We have been before God's throne and back." We all felt the awe of God's holiness.

I love that friend who had confronted me with truth in such a tragic time, for indeed, he was a *true* friend. A true friend will speak the truth no matter how hard or inappropriate it may seem. He had been the voice of severe mercy to me, and in that, there is love. Speaking truth requires the sacrifice of self-preservation. Jesus said to His close followers, "Greater love has no man than this, that he lay down his life for his friends." This man had been courageous and loving enough to do that for me. He had taken the risk of my fierce reaction, anger, and rejection, and put himself at jeopardy for my sake.

The repenting that I went through during that hour was for my benefit—to transform me and change me from water to wine, not to change God's plan, not to control God or manipulate Him, and not to cause a miracle of my own imagining. The repenting was to get me to a place of total surrender from my will to His. To surrender was the only hope available for my brokenness. I came to the place where I was willing for God to *be* God and I trusted Him . . . His love and His healing.

Faith at times seems unreasonable, but it is not mindless. Respected pastor Bill Johnson wrote, *"Faith is superior to reason in that it gives our intellect a context in which to grow safely. Trust makes us powerful."* God's love is powerful enough to change water to wine, and ordinary hope into extraordinary faith!

Words for Reflection

"Despite all my emotions, I will believe and praise the One who saves me, my God" (Psalm 42:11 Voice).

There is never any benefit in giving up hope in the Lord.

"A *true* friend loves regardless of the situation, and a *real* brother exists to share the tough times" (Proverbs 17:17 Voice).

It takes guts to be a real friend and not become offended.

I want to be a true friend—to be real, truthful, and without offense.

Family Forgiveness . . . and Then the Crash

Late in the afternoon on that same day, Steve and I gathered with our daughters at a friend's house, and we had our own time for family forgiveness. We spoke forgiveness to each other for our individual failures related to Andrew's accident. Our guilt fell largely in the realm of things that *should* have been done. Omission is no less painful or gripping than the sin that is committed intentionally—it is still sin and needs to be forgiven, so that freedom from guilt can be experienced. Forgiveness doesn't deny that problems or misunderstandings occur. Rather, it annihilates the power of accusation and condemnation in our future.

One of our friends had advised Steve to build a fence around our swimming pool, but I didn't want the fence—it cluttered up my landscape design. Steve believed we should have a fence, but he procrastinated in building it.

As we gathered as a family, Steve led the way by asking us to forgive him for not building a fence around the pool. We each spoke forgiveness in simple, direct words—"I forgive you." Any failure was put fully under Christ's blood once and for all during that time.

> *Forgiveness annihilates the power of accusation and condemnation in our future.*
>
>

Ten-year-old Jessica asked for forgiveness for not watching Andrew more closely that afternoon when he was playing by the pool. Who would have ever anticipated that after an entire summer by the pool without any mishaps, on that particular day he would have fallen into the pool? We spoke our forgiveness fully and freely to Jessica, and any negligence on her part was placed under the blood of Jesus, never to be brought up again.

Seven-year-old Rebekah asked for forgiveness for her selfishness in not wanting to stop playing when she saw Andrew by the pool. Forgiveness was granted fully and freely, and the incident was forever placed under Christ's blood, never to be mentioned again by any of us.

I asked for forgiveness for not wanting a fence—oh, the foolishness of vanity. Once again, forgiveness was granted.

The power of forgiveness healed each one of us that day, as only forgiveness combined with love can do.

This time of family forgiveness was a golden key in unlocking the deep feelings we experienced in our own unique ways. If we had not released those feelings in confession to one another and received words of forgiveness, we could have each been locked into grief, bitterness, and blame for the rest of our lives. Steve prayed and declared that all of our faults were under the blood of Jesus. We were forgiven by the Lord and we had forgiven each other. Guilt, shame, and blame had no power or future with our family.

And that has been the case. We have lived freely, both individually and as a family. To this day, not one time have our failures been mentioned again to another in our family—there is no blame, no guilt, and no shame. We each learned that forgiveness is a powerful weapon against Satan, for it removes all potential for bitterness. I cannot remember one time that any of us have referred to Andrew's death in an accusatory way.

> *Through the spoken act of forgiveness, we had removed any ground that Satan might have used to torment us for the rest of our lives.*
>
>

As soon as we finished this precious family time, we got a call from the hospital asking that Steve and I come back to the hospital as quickly as we could. Andrew had "crashed" and all of his physical systems were shutting down. We left the girls at our friend's house and rushed to Andrew's room.

The Crash

God had stayed the hand of death until we each had time to make things right with one another in our family and with Him. Through the spoken act of forgiveness, we had removed any ground that Satan might have used to torment us for the rest of our lives, tearing our marriage and our family apart through blame and if-only thinking. Our failures had been forgiven and God fulfilled his promise to remove them as far as the east is from the west. Grounds for any accusation from any source had been annihilated through our forgiveness.

As we raced back to the hospital in silence, I felt stunned and bewildered by my thoughts and emotions. Yes, I had said to God, "Not my will, but your will, Lord." Yes, I had agreed that if it was God's will to take Andrew, I yielded to that. Yes, I still had hope in the Lord to heal and restore Andrew to us. Yes, yes, yes. I stood firm in my faith for a miracle, and yet, deep within I found myself hoping. "Somehow, I thought you would come through, Lord. I am not ready for Andrew to leave us," I thought. The reality of his death flooded my soul, and I didn't see how I could bear it.

The crash had involved a cessation of brain activity. The doctors had already put Andrew on life support, but now, from a medical point of view, Andrew was brain-dead.

As much as the pediatrician tried to make sense of the unexpected crash, Steve and I both knew that the greater truth was simply that our heavenly Father had not chosen to allow Andrew to remain on earth with us, but had instead chosen to take him home to be with Him—just as ten-year-old Jessica had quietly explained during our first night in the hospital.

It took three more days for confirmation tests to be done. Beyond that, we needed to make the decision to remove Andrew from *all* life-support systems—that decision was ours alone to make. I found myself quietly whispering to the Lord, "Okay, Lord, you say your grace is sufficient for all our needs. This is a giant one!" I knew in my spirit that Andrew had already departed to be with Jesus, but as long as his little body was still warm and his heart showed a beat on a monitor, there seemed to be a part of Andrew I could still hold on to.

The Lord continued to reveal Himself through the amazing and abundant grace poured out through various people around us. My oldest brother, Chuck, had taken time off from his medical practice to be there with us. He did not say very much that week; he mainly drove me early in the morning to the hospital and then back home late at night. He carried our Bibles in and out of the hospital. He was there with us, he prayed, and that was grace sufficient. God also provided great grace through our pediatrician who came to our home to tell us about the final test results—a kind and gracious act that we had not expected. Many friends and neighbors took care of all our physical needs—from mowing our large lawn and cleaning the house to cutting Chuck's hair and preparing food for our family. People also came by just to comfort us. God's love poured out in very practical and ordinary ways, all of which were exceedingly profound to us and greatly appreciated.

Two more days passed and there was no change in Andrew's physical condition. I fought the idea that Andrew might be lying on his deathbed. I knew that Jesus could raise the dead, and I was still unable or unwilling to see Andrew die.

The story of the widow's son in Nain was a classic example of God raising up a mother's son to life, even as he was being carried on a pallet to his grave (Luke 7:11–17).

The story of Lazarus, who had been wrapped in burial clothes and laid in a tomb for four days only to be "called forth" by Jesus to new life was another strong biblical example of Jesus raising the dead (John 11:38–44).

And certainly, the most profound story in the Bible about resurrection is the resurrection of Jesus Himself, crucified and buried only to rise from the dead three days later (Matthew 28:1–8).

I recalled the statement that Jesus made to Martha outside of the tomb of Lazarus. Jesus had asked Martha whether she believed in the resurrection. She had answered with a qualified yes, saying, "Yes, in the last days." But what was that supposed to mean to *me* as I waited just a few yards away from my son lying on a bed in the ICU? Jesus responded to her, *"I am the resurrection and the life."* Jesus made a strong claim to be the One who held and imparted resurrection life at all times—not just after death. But, I wanted that *now* form of resurrection for Andrew, and I wanted it with my whole heart.

> *Once someone has seen Jesus, a whole new dimension of love occurs in that person's heart and carries them into places and service perhaps not previously expected.*

I wanted the timing of Andrew's resurrection to be immediate. I wanted him to be resurrected to live on this earth. I did not want to even consider that Jesus would resurrect Andrew in a way that would result in Andrew immediately going to be with Him in heaven. I wanted him to grow up into manhood, get married, and have the joy of children. I wanted a full life for him on earth with his family—he had barely begun to live out his wonderful life.

I saw his life with Steve, me, and his sisters as the best possible resurrected life for Andrew. I had totally discounted—truly, I had not even considered—the glories of a resurrected life for Andrew into the presence of Jesus. I knew that would come someday . . . not just now. Jessica was right when she said that first night in the hospital, "Andrew has seen Jesus. He doesn't want to come back home." Once someone has seen Jesus, a whole new dimension of love occurs in that person's heart and carries them into places and service perhaps not previously expected.

Is Jesus the resurrection? Does He give a resurrected life to all who die in Christ? Is the resurrected life Jesus gives the one that transports us into eternity?

The answer is absolutely *yes!*

I wish I could say that I embraced this firm and resolute conclusion with inward and outward peace while waiting in the hospital's hallways, but I did not. The early church embraced this truth so that all could say, "O death, where is your sting?" (1 Corinthians 15:55).

It was through the grace of God and love shown by those who stood with me and our family during these days at the hospital that I finally felt enabled and empowered to agree with the final decision to release Andrew's body from all life-support systems on Friday morning, assuming that this would only happen should a great miracle not happen first.

The decision gave me one final night to be by Andrew's hospital bed, to hold my baby boy and talk with him. It was one final night to voice all the prayers left within me, asking for a miracle. I needed grace and strength, but I also needed to be faithful to what I had heard. I found myself saying repeatedly, "Though you slay me, yet will I hope in you, Lord." I had hated hearing those words from Steve just five days earlier and I still hated them, but there was no alternative. I had to choose hope!

> *I needed to come to the place where I could say, apart from any circumstances now and forever, "I trust you."*
>
>

In those final hours of tears and prayer, I kept looking for another possibility that might be easier and less painful. I cried out, "Anything but death, Lord!" The truth is, there was no path to greater life for Andrew except through death. In many ways, I was crying out to my heavenly Father for my life as much as for Andrew's. *I needed to see beyond this earthly existence into eternity and come to the place, once again, of believing and embracing life after death, and this time, for my son. I needed to be able to breathe in God's peace and truly mean the words, "Not my will be done, but your will."* How did Jesus say those very words in Gethsemane His last day on earth? Grace! God's grace is the most powerful gift on this earth.

How did Jesus pray such a prayer with no conditions attached? How did He *fully* yield all trust to the Father? Truly, trust was, and still is, the bottom line. I needed to come to the place where I could say, apart from any circumstances now and forever, "I trust you."

I would never presume to equate my last night with Andrew to Jesus' last night in Gethsemane, yet, I had a knowing that Jesus fully understood my pain and heart cry.

In a book by Gene Edwards, he explains that Gethsemane is the place where divinity and frail humanity come into agreement; where a person comes into agreement with the Father. The idea of our frail humanity coming into agreement with the all-powerful, all-wise God is a tremendous mystery, but one that I know to be true and possible.

We gathered for one more time of prayer. At that point, we were not praying for healing, but for true resurrection from the dead. We prayed late into the night.

That final night, the doctors' dining room was unusually quiet. Several people were there during every hour. Some sang softly and prayed, but overall, the atmosphere was one of somber reality and a quiet strengthening.

I left no room in my heart for what-if—the greatest tactic of remorse and regret!

I know there were people at the hospital who took pity on us, and perhaps, thought we were a little weird or even crazy. One of our young friends, a pastor, came to Andrew's room where some of us were gathered to pray. He walked in, took off his shoes, laid prostrate on the floor, and began praying loudly for Andrew's life to be raised up. He prayed this over and over again. I found myself wondering, "What will people think?" He was praying so loudly that I was sure his voice could be heard all the way down the hospital corridor and into the rooms of other patients. Looking back, I have thought many times about how this young man completely humbled himself on our behalf . . . and I was embarrassed? I am so grateful for those whose faith rules over the opinion of men.

Who cares what people think? But then again, I was worried about my reputation! I am always astounded that such conflicting thoughts can bombard a mind at the same time. This was my son, my only son, and I thought to myself, "I *will* join my young friend and cry out to God in heaven!" I left no room in my heart for what-if—the greatest tactic of remorse and regret!

I humbly begged God, even though I didn't expect anything different than the reality of what was before me. Such dichotomy in my thoughts—such double-mindedness!

It takes guts to cry out loud in an atmosphere or place where it has been deemed improper. It takes guts to praise in the face of death. That night I ceased, once again, to care what anybody thought—which made me think of Matthew 11:12.

As I stood in faith, trusting a merciful God, I found myself looking beyond what I saw in my mind. I caught a glimpse of the resurrection. I caught a glimpse of Andrew's life in eternity.

When morning dawned, there was no beautiful sunrise, only stark reality. There had been no before-death resurrection during the night. God wanted us to release Andrew into His eternal arms. *Now was the time for God's grace and strength to be resurrected within my soul and body.*

Words for Reflection

Jesus prayed, "My Father, if it is possible, may this cup be taken from me. Yet not as I will, but as you will" (Matthew 26:39 NIV).

Jesus did not pray this prayer from feelings—He prayed it from faith, truth, and commitment. And He prayed it from love.

The Holy Spirit always desires to enable and empower us to pray as Jesus prayed.

"But when He, the Spirit of truth, comes, He will guide you into all the truth; for He will not speak on His own initiative, but whatever He hears, He will speak; and He will disclose to you what is to come" (John 16:13 NASB).

"The mind set on the Spirit is life and peace" (Romans 8:6 NASB).

"Forgive, and you will be forgiven" (Luke 6:37).

9

Saying Good-Bye

The dreaded Friday morning came. Death was imminent. Eight days had passed since we brought Andrew to the hospital. This was his final morning in that sacred hospital room.

For the last time, I made my way down the long, familiar corridor to Andrew's room, where Steve and the girls were already waiting for me. Tears were rushing down my cheeks, my heart was pounding, and my mind was whirling. I kept asking myself silently, *"Are we doing the right thing? Did we have enough faith? What if we are making a mistake?"* Doubts and fears came as an onslaught.

Just when I thought I could bear no more, I heard God speak gently, **"Look beyond what you see and fix your eyes on Jesus, the author and perfecter of your faith."**

"What?" I silently asked the Lord. "How do I look beyond the confusion, the dashed hopes, the looming fears, and make sense out of the utter confusion and despair of my messed-up heart?"

I tried to understand what I heard, but it made no earthly sense. "No, Lord, what I see and what I must do seem impossible! How can I allow them to unhook him from the machines that are keeping him alive? How can I do that? I am his mother! God, do something! Please do anything, as long as it is something! To take Andrew off of life support is issuing his death warrant! This is asking too much, Father. Help me!"

> *God was not playing a mind game to get me to deny the reality I saw; He was coaching me to stay hopeful, to embrace my future instead of forfeiting it.*
>
>

The Lord continued, *"Don't look at the obvious. Look at me. Keep your eyes on me. I will help you."*

God was not playing a mind game to get me to deny the reality I saw; He was coaching me to stay hopeful, to embrace my future instead of forfeiting it. My Father in heaven was trying to get me to focus on Him, just the way I did with my daughters when I needed them to hear and understand me clearly. I often said, "Girls, look at me! I'll not go on talking until you look at me and listen." Father God was trying to get me to look at Him and draw upon the faith He had deposited and cultivated in me from the time of my salvation experience. *Faith would allow me to see beyond this earth's reality, and faith would bear me up.*

Suddenly, mysteriously, I felt as though I was being lifted two or three feet off the corridor floor. I finished the walk to Andrew's room feeling like I was elevated above the circumstances—the Lord was now carrying me! I was no longer bearing my burden, and my fear was fleeing. Doubt was giving way to trust. With my focus fully on Jesus, the mighty and tender "perfecter," my faith was being transformed and was calming my frenzied and frayed soul. My ragged emotions that had been stretched to the limit, tossed to and fro, were now being soothed. A mind battered with unrelenting speculations and fears was becoming focused and steadfast. And a will that was worn and weary was being strengthened.

Within those few minutes, I truly began to *believe* that we would make it through this great sorrow without being demolished as a couple and as a family. We were going to make it because Jesus was carrying us!

As a family, we gathered to say good-bye to Andrew. Steve sat by Andrew's crib, played his guitar, and worshipped the Lord.

My brother Chuck, our nephew Chase, and our daughter Jessica wanted to stay in the room with Steve while the doctor and nurse unhooked Andrew's body from life support. I did not want to stay—I did not have the grace to stay. They remained there while the rest of us left the room. When we returned to the room, we saw him lying there, wrapped in his favorite yellow "blankie," with his favorite lamb stuffed animal by his side. All of the tubes and noisy machines were gone. All was quiet. I picked up his little body and held him in my arms and rocked him. His body began to feel just as it had the day that I lifted him from the swimming pool—lifeless, limp, and cold.

Steve then took Andrew in his arms and lifted his precious body above his head. Loudly, he spoke God's word back to the heavens, *"Though you slay us, yet will we hope in you!"* This truly was Steve's sacrifice of praise. When he lifted up our son, he lifted up his praise. He surrendered the right to understand and shifted into a higher realm of faith.

> *Our hope is never in what we experience, our hope is in Jesus. Only then is our hope steadfast when the storms of life violently crash against us.*

Every person in the room cried and was witness to this holy moment of giving. We, in turn, received God's mercy which would comfort and sustain us in the hours, days, and months ahead. Again, as Pastor Bill Johnson wrote, *"True faith is superior to reason in that it gives our intellect a context in which to grow safely."*

Our hope is never in what we experience, our hope is in Jesus. Only then is our hope steadfast when the storms of life violently crash against us.

We stepped outside of our son's hospital room and greeted the friends who had gathered there. We simply told them, "We are going home." I turned one last time to look at my son with his little lamb beside him, knowing that Andrew had already gone home. The nurse, a dear friend, wrapped Andrew up in his soft, yellow blanket, held his body in her arms, and waited in a quiet hallway until the attendants from the funeral home came to pick up his body. What would we do without friends?

We were driven home by some of our other friends, where family and more friends were gathered to welcome and comfort us. More and more people kept arriving that evening. Ronda, a close friend and gifted pianist, arrived from a city a couple of hours away. The Lord had spoken to her, "Go to the Swift's home. Play the piano and worship me." That's exactly what happened. We pressed ourselves into the music room of our home and sang and worshiped the Lord well into the night.

Outside, another friend had built a campfire near our pond and gathered all of the children to play quietly and roast hot dogs. This was the same friend who had confronted me in the hospital. A true friend will walk the second mile with you, even if it might be risky or costly.

Without us knowing it, yet another friend had gone to the funeral home where he asked to see Andrew's body. He laid hands on Andrew's body and prayed one more time for him to be raised from the dead. It was a dear act of faith and commitment on his part, and to us, an act of great love.

The following day, a small group of friends and family waited for us at the grave site. One of the men who carried Andrew's small casket had also carried the casket of Grace Ann, our daughter. Faithful God and faithful friends—we need them both.

We did not have Andrew's body embalmed because we wanted to pray for resurrection until his little coffin was lowered into the ground. We invited a small group of like-minded Christian friends to pray and to cry out to the Lord with us. There at the open grave we prayed and we worshipped, but Andrew was not resurrected on this earth.

At Andrew's grave site, we quietly laid his body into the earth.

The next afternoon, a Sunday, we held the memorial service at First Baptist Church in honor of Stephen Andrew Swift. The sanctuary was filled to the brim with friends, family, neighbors, business acquaintances, doctors, and nurses. The glory of God's presence was there, and we felt His great comfort.

In the days, weeks, and even months following Andrew's death, I began to comprehend the full magnitude of the battle that we had experienced during Andrew's stay in the hospital. It was more than a battle for *his* life—it was a war over what thoughts and beliefs would control *our* lives and the future of our family. The Bible tells us, "As a man thinks in his heart, so is he." It is our thoughts that define our view of life—our values, attitudes, and ultimately, our beliefs. It is our thoughts that give rise to our feelings of being hopeless or hopeful, faithless or faithful, and joyless or joyful. It is within our minds that we fight the battles for truth, by which we will make all of life's choices. We are given the mind of Christ at our salvation. It is trusting God alone that makes us powerful and fearless.

It was in the fiery trial associated with Andrew's death that we made the pure choices that would not only last the rest of our lives, but for all of eternity.

Words for Reflection

In King David's prayers after his son died, he said, "I shall go to him, but he shall not return to me" (2 Samuel 12:23).

This is the hope of all godly parents who have surrendered a beloved child to the Father in heaven: we will go to be with our child in heaven someday!

"I am the resurrection and the source of all life; those who believe in Me will live even in death. Everyone who lives and believes in Me will never truly die. Do you believe this?" (John 11:25–26 Voice).

Do you believe this? In times of despair or crisis, this cannot be faked.

10

A *Point* of *No Return*

We said good-bye to Andrew knowing that we had exercised the best of our faith, asking for the ultimate miracle. Knowing that we had given our all, we were able to fully and peacefully release Andrew to the Lord.

When deep tragedy and sorrow overwhelm us, we find that nothing really seems to matter except the love of those close to us and the love of God.

Emotions are fragile, and joy felt utterly elusive to us. But bit by bit, as we allowed the grace of God to infuse us anew, we each found, in different ways, the truth that we would once more experience a day when we could laugh and live joyously. We began to breathe again.

Each one of us attempted to cope with the tragedy of Andrew's death in our own way, and later on, we also understood that God was preparing each of us for a life that was redeemed above sorrow, in His timing and in His way.

I have witnessed instant healing and I have witnessed healing that took place over time. The truth is, Jesus still heals today, but it is in His way and on His timetable—He is God! He understands our past, our present, and our future.

> *When deep tragedy and sorrow overwhelm us, we find that nothing really seems to matter except the love of those close to us and the love of God.*

In the aftermath of Andrew's death and burial, Steve and I made a commitment to venture out beyond anything that sounded emotionally logical to us, or even humanly possible. We told God that we would belong to Him in service, praise, and devotion, regardless of what had happened or what anyone thought. We wanted to believe and trust even more in the God of mercy, whose ways are higher. We laid down all bargaining.

Balms of Praise and Fellowship

The following Sunday after Andrew's memorial service, a group of friends showed up at our home and announced to us that they were there "to have church." Steve and I hardly knew how to respond. We had just buried Andrew only the week before, and we were not in any position to lead anything. They did not ask or expect us to. They simply came to our home to be together, to worship, and to pray. We invited them in.

We assumed that this was a one-time Sunday event, but the next Sunday even more people showed up. Added to the group was my realtor friend and her husband, and both the builder of our home and the electrician who had installed the wiring. In all, we were a diverse group, but this was something God was establishing in His timing, and we all sensed that.

We kept meeting, week after week, in our home. Then we moved into a large, empty rental house loaned to us by our realtor friend. It was in that rental house on one cold night that we gathered in the kitchen around an open oven for warmth. As we were sharing our needs with each other, Steve described his emotional pain by comparing it to a "cannonball hole" that he felt had been shot into his chest and heart. So we prayed for healing. Nothing out of the ordinary happened during the prayer time, and we said good-bye and went home. The next morning when Steve woke up, he looked at me and said, "It's gone! The hole is gone!" *Just like that! A miraculous healing came through the prayers of ordinary believers in Jesus Christ.*

About a month after we buried Andrew, I felt like I had crashed. I could not seem to pull myself out of feelings of hopelessness and despair. I felt forsaken and I was depressed. One morning, I walked into our kitchen and said aloud, "Lord, does anyone remember me? Does anyone even remember what I've been through and care what I feel like today?" In the next moment, the phone rang and the voice on the other end of the line said, "Judy, I'm calling just to let you know that I am still praying for you and your family and to tell you that you are not forgotten." Coincidence? I don't think so!

More time passed and I felt that I needed a change of scenery. The house, Andrew's empty nursery, and the homeschooling responsibilities all began to close in on me. I needed to get away for a weekend, so I went to my mother-in-law's home in Tyler, Texas—her home felt like a sanctuary.

I packed up Jessica and Rebekah and took them to a friend's farm that had cows and horses. And, my friend was even willing to substitute teach! I knew my daughters would have fun there, and I believed that my time away would allow Steve to catch up on his work without feeling any responsibility for me or the girls for a few days. All of the pieces seemed to fall into place for that time away.

While in Tyler, I attended my sister-in-law's Bible study, which had about one hundred women attending it. Most of the women in the group had prayed for Andrew and for our family, and they asked me to share if I wanted to. As I was sharing about the faithfulness and mercy of the Lord, I experienced a physical sensation that felt as if warm oil was being poured over my head. It trickled all the way down my body to my feet. *It was such a real sensation that it felt as if the oil was truly going to puddle on the floor around my feet.* I stopped speaking for a few seconds, and I looked at the floor beneath my feet. There was nothing there. A bit shaken, I quickly ended my sharing and sat down. It was amazing, but I told no one about this experience—perhaps, I thought it too holy, or more likely, I didn't know how to explain it. So, I tucked the experience away in my heart.

When I returned home several days later and walked through the back door, I hugged and kissed Steve. *Immediately he said, "You have experienced healing. You are different."*

Healing—that was it! He was absolutely right. The *invisible* oil that the Holy Spirit poured out on me took on a *visible* manifestation of change in my physical being and soul. The depression and heaviness were gone! I began to *feel* and, in turn, act in a way that reflected a restoration of my heart. It was truly a divine miracle of healing from an amazing God!

Steve, Jessica, Rebekah, and I were being made whole again, and joy was returning to our wonderful little family.

As our Sunday group continued meeting together, we also witnessed other miracles. We regularly saw marriages heal and salvations occur. Money was given to help the poor, and every need in our tiny gathering was met, down to the Lord providing a volunteer nursery worker. Amazing grace and provision for such a time! Perhaps, in the back of all of our minds, we were wondering when this heaven on earth would end and we would return to our previous, respective churches.

Our expression of "church" had no pastor, but we shared teachings. We didn't gather around a man, but rather, around the Word of God. Powerful speakers from large churches in other cities came to speak at our gatherings without a guaranteed payment but love offerings only. How does this sort of thing happen so easily? It was the hand of a miracle-working God who was invited and welcomed in our midst.

Our praise and worship and our love for one another was church. Looking back, I believe that in a very brief time, our expectations about what a church should be had been changed by the Lord. Our gathering was truly an earthly expression of God's promise that He will give beauty for ashes, which He did not only for our family, but for all who gathered together.

Words for Reflection

"I have been crucified with Christ; and it is no longer I who live, but Christ lives in me; and the life which I now live in the flesh I live by faith in the Son of God, who loved me and gave Himself up for me" (Galatians 2:20 NASB).

What persons you loved, dreams, hopes, or relationships in your life have died or ended?

What life has come out of that death? What life have you asked for from the Father who always gives goodness . . . joy for sorrow?

Ask Him now!

11

Becoming Official

There were about twenty families who made the "wilderness trek" with us from our home to the empty rental house each week, and then as we outgrew that, to the empty church facility that we leased. When that space was sold, we leased another church facility. At last, a small Methodist church facility in the heart of the city went on the market.

We made the decision to purchase that property, which was a major step of faith and courage, since we had such a small number of people who were willing to give the needed funds. Of the twenty or so families we had at the time of the purchase, three were single-parent families and two families were unemployed. From a financial standpoint, we were unimpressive, but nevertheless, we were a faithful people who trusted in a faithful God.

After much prayer, we negotiated with the owner of the property and we specified three criteria that had to be met for us to take possession of our "promised land." We needed for the owner to reduce the price by 25 percent, we needed the bank to loan us the mortgage amount as a group, without any individuals signing as surety, and we agreed to pay fifty thousand dollars as a down payment within thirty days. This was a staggering amount to our small band, so we prayed and agreed on a very simple fund-raising program. We decided to tell everyone in our group how much money we needed, to read aloud 2 Corinthians 9:7, which tells us that each one should give as he purposes in his own heart, to ask each family to pray about the amount to give, and then to share that commitment with us the next Sunday.

When the following Sunday came, we had six inches of snow in Fort Smith and we could not meet. We called all of the families and asked them to write down the amount that God had spoken to them to give, place that number in an envelope, and mail it to us. We asked that they not put their name or any return address on the letter—their commitment was to the Lord, not to us.

When we finally met a week later, we had all of the envelopes at the front of the church. The room was charged with excitement! Some of the men took the envelopes to one side of the sanctuary and began to open them and tally the amount.

As they were doing this, a single woman who had arrived late came down the aisle, and said, "I did not get to mail the amount in to you, but here it is." She handed Steve a note with "$1,000" written on it. The men soon finished their tally and brought the final number to Steve. They had counted $49,000. Steve then handed them the woman's note with the $1,000 commitment, which brought the total to exactly $50,000! We were in awe and we were in!

It was a miracle at one level that our small group could even commit that much money, but for the commitment at the one gathering time to be exactly the fifty thousand dollars that we needed was truly more than astonishing. We shouted and praised the Lord and celebrated.

Doesn't this sum up the kingdom of God? Life out of death, forgiveness instead of condemnation.

A few months later, after all the papers were signed and the money was given, the beautiful building in the center of the city with the big trees was officially ours. As we were taking ownership of our place, the Lord gave us the name for our fellowship: City Christian Fellowship.

How appropriate this name was! We were Christians now located in the heart of a city, and fellowship was a perfect description of our relationship with one another. We were becoming known for our love and our response to those who were hurting and in need.

This was truly our church now. It was a church birthed out of the death of Andrew. The Sunday that we moved in was full of rejoicing, and the thought filled my mind that I was getting to see a glimpse of what heaven is like—praise, worship, and such joy. I knew with renewed certainty that Andrew was experiencing that same atmosphere fully and constantly in heaven. He was living in the very atmosphere of resurrected life.

Doesn't this sum up the kingdom of God? Life out of death, forgiveness instead of condemnation. We were a group of believers seeking joy through worship and service, peace through forgiveness and healing, and righteousness through being transformed by the power of the Holy Spirit.

Prior to our first service in our new facility, all of the families gathered and prepared the buildings and grounds for us to move in. We met for the first time in the building on the first Sunday in July of 1988. Steve preached a message on "crossing the Jordan" from the book of Joshua. At the end of the message, he asked the head of each family to symbolically bring a stone to the front of the sanctuary. This was to be our "altar of Gilgal" as a remembrance of the great and wonderful things our God had done on behalf of all of us.

One man and his wife were visiting with their family that first Sunday. They were so touched by the presence of God, the joyful celebration, and the significance of this symbolic sacrificial act that they stood up and carried to the front a very large imaginary stone that was laid at the altar. Along with the laying of the stone, they immediately joined our fellowship from that day forward. The entire service was marked by a tremendous atmosphere of commitment and thanksgiving.

Miracles became more common. Marriages were strengthened and children were meeting Jesus in wondrous ways. I had never experienced anything like it, nor have I since. It was a time when friends and acquaintances experienced the powerful presence of God together; and together, we were all becoming more like Jesus.

One day, we invited a pastor from England to be a guest speaker. When he and Steve entered the door of the sanctuary, this man stopped, saying, "Wait for just a while." He wanted to fully take in what he was seeing—the gathering, talking, and laughter of the people and the tuning of guitars. Steve had talked to him about putting together bylaws, an order of worship, and other things that most churches have. As this man stood quietly observing, he finally said, "The God we all worship makes every snowflake different. God is doing something new here, something different. Don't rush to be like others. God is making you different—it is refreshing and inspiring."

In very real ways, the church that grew from the fellowship in our home—which was a fellowship that was birthed out of the gathering together of those who had prayed diligently and powerfully for Andrew and for us in the aftermath of Andrew's death—was a church birthed *because* of what had happened with Andrew. What the Devil had meant as death, God used as the kernel that birthed new life, and for many through the years, eternal life.

As we experienced such unabashed and unorthodox responses to the calling of the Lord on us, we began the next phase of our journey together. Almost overnight, new people began to come to our beautiful little church in the center of the city. It became a lighthouse of praise and worship and a stronghold for prayer and healing. It was a refuge of love and acceptance to all who ventured into the building and became distinguished by us and others as a place filled with the presence of the Lord.

We increased in favor with God, men, and in the realm of worship through the arts. Three women (I was one of them) had previously written a small drama, *A Son Is Given*. Later we revised it with added music, dance, and magnificent costumes, and performed it in a little theater called The King Opera House. It became our church's privilege to give this anointed presentation as a free gift to our city and surrounding towns for the next three years. The blessing and reputation of the play increased until the performances had standing room only.

A double album, *Behind the Veil*, was written by Craig Smith, a singer and songwriter in our fellowship. We also transformed the albums into a musical-drama experience. The church created the dance, drama, and costumes, while Craig sang the songs and the Lord poured out His magnificent anointing. The production was performed in cities throughout Northwest Arkansas, Louisiana, Alabama, Kentucky, and even in Jamaica.

We saw the salvation and baptism of many in our midst, and we even developed a tradition of allowing fathers to baptize their own children after the children had accepted Jesus as their Savior. We saw miracles of healing, the restoration of broken relationships, and a steady growth in people and in knowledge of the Word of God.

Prior to Andrew's birth, I had been given three prophetic words by three different people from three different cities, all of which said that Andrew's life would be used to bring people to the Lord. One prophetic word even referred to "thousands" who would come to Christ. Our church, City Christian

Fellowship, was birthed out of Andrew's death, and through these two dramas alone, I would suppose that thousands have been told the truth of Jesus Christ through the Word of God, song, and drama. And with those thousands, the prophetic words given concerning Andrew's young life have come to pass.

Many of those who gathered with us at the hospital at the time of Andrew's death became members of our new church fellowship. They all knew the full story of Andrew's birth, life, and death, and of God's work in our lives as his parents and with his sisters. They saw the Lord's healing work in us, and it truly became a part of their witness in telling about the Lord, about our church fellowship, and about God's loving presence to all who would believe— no matter the harshness of circumstances or the sorrow of situations.

Some of those who were deeply and eternally touched by Andrew's death knew Andrew in some way, while others who were impacted by his life never even met him.

It wasn't the way we had thought God would fulfill His prophetic word, but it was God's way. In a very real way, Andrew and his story are still touching lives, including those who read this book and might go on to tell others about his life and death and the miraculous aftermath. Even beyond what I might see or know in the natural, there is an eternity of meaning to Andrew's life that is still unfolding in God's presence, and none of us can truly know the plans and purposes that God is working out on the other side of death's veil.

Did Andrew's life have meaning for all eternity—far beyond anything we could know? Most assuredly!

Words for Reflection

"'For I know the plans I have for you,' declares the Lord, 'plans to prosper you and not to harm you, plans to give you hope and a future. Then you will call on me and come and pray to me, and I will listen to you'" (Jeremiah 29:11–12 NIV).

"But I trust in you, Lord; I say, 'You are my God.' My times are in your hands" (Psalm 31:14-15 NIV).

"May he give you the desire of your heart and make all your plans succeed. May we shout for joy over your victory and lift up our banners in the name of our God. May the Lord grant all your requests" (Psalm 20:4–5 NIV).

"Your overflowing goodness You have kept for those who live in awe of You, And You share Your goodness with those who make You their sanctuary" (Psalm 31:19 Voice).

Confessing what God has said on our behalf is a powerful act of recovery and redemption.

◇ 12 ◇

The Wonder of Hearing God's Voice

Do you believe God speaks to human beings? And more importantly, do you believe He speaks to *you*?

I believe both. I believe he speaks to humans and I know that He speaks to me, as I have already shared some of my experiences with hearing the voice of God. I believe our "hearing from God" is vital to our understanding of the reality of His presence and power in our personal lives. We are able to receive divine direction for how *God* desires that we live. The Bible gives us these simple words about hearing the Lord's voice:

> *I believe our "hearing from God" is vital to our understanding of the reality of His presence and power in our personal lives.*
>
> ↰

"He will surely be gracious to you at the sound of your cry; when He hears it, He will answer you. Your ears will hear a word behind you, 'This is the way, walk in it'" (Isaiah 30:19, 21 NASB).

"My sheep hear My voice" (John 10:27 NASB). This was the scripture I painted on Andrew's nursery wall.

Two *Preferable* Prerequisites: Desire and Stillness

For me, there seem to be two main prerequisites for hearing God's voice—the first is a quiet desire, or in my case in the hospital, a desperate desire, to hear it. That is not always as obvious as it may sound. Many people either don't believe God speaks to individual human beings in our modern world today, or they believe they are not worthy or spiritual enough. Some simply are satisfied with sticking to the status quo in their relationship with God. Others have no expectation of something more, and perhaps others fear that God won't say what they want Him to say. Could a lack of desire to hear the Lord be erroneously based on a lie that God is not a good Father because of a negative earthly experience? We often do not listen to those who we don't know, don't trust, or feel will hurt us.

The second prerequisite for hearing God's voice is stillness. God's Word challenges us to be still and know God—not only know about Him, but truly *know* Him. In a number of cases in the Bible, the Lord's voice is described as a still, small voice that comes to the deepest part of a person's spirit. The Lord tells us that He will answer us in the secret place of thunder (see Psalm 81:7). The Lord speaks to us through His written Word, the Bible. To be still before the Lord requires that we intentionally shut out all of the superfluous noise around us that would distract us—including cell phones, computers, radios, and TVs.

It is a purposeful maneuver to establish quiet times. Eastern religions and Judaism refer to quiet times as meditation. I do believe in meditation, but I usually begin with just reading the Bible until *something* registers and gets my attention. Then, I'll stop and get still. I'll think on that passage of the Bible or the thought that caught my heart while I was reading, and then I'll just wait, in order to give the Lord a chance to speak. We must train ourselves to really tune in. Be attentive to the impressions and to the parts of the Bible that seem to leap off the page. Expect to hear a whispering thought. This is putting our faith into action.

God Is Personal

My relationship with Jesus began with my hearing His voice. Remember when I was presenting the gospel to a stranger for the first time? When I got to the part where I was to say, "All you have to do is transfer all your trust from yourself to Jesus Christ alone to save you," I heard God's voice say to me, ***"But you have never done this."*** His voice was so real that I became discombobulated. I stopped and looked around to see who was speaking. I was undone to the point that my trainer had to finish the gospel presentation.

I had clearly heard His voice. It redirected the course of my life. From that moment forward, I have focused my life and my soul to hear God's voice. I have practiced, anticipated, and asked over and over for Him to speak to me anytime and anywhere. *It is about having a relationship.*

His voice and His written Word have literally saved my life, redirected my course, and changed my thinking. I can't imagine what it would be like not to hear Him or speak to Him and know that He has heard me—that He has heard my heart cry and my expressed joy. When the eternal God speaks, what He says is eternal—it is for always and for all situations. *His Word does not cease with time.*

> *The God of this universe and of our lives does not conform Himself to us, but rather, we are conformed to Him.*
>
>

God's Word is not only eternal and for all people, it is also extremely personal. Unfortunately, our educational system and religious system attempt to produce conformity rather than creativity and personal application. Even so, the God of this universe and of our lives does not conform Himself to us, but rather, we are conformed to Him.

If we cannot come to God with all our heart, give Him all of our cares and fears, then we will be bound to *less than* and not *more than*. Christ in us is the hope of glory. We must learn to drink from our own well of faith. That well will contain our eternal experiences with God that never seem to run dry. He is eternal—He is *never ending*. His words spoken to us personally or through the Bible have the same dynamics and power they had thousands of years ago. *He is the eternal God.*

When I gave Jesus my heart when I was in my twenties, He took ownership and promised me eternal life. He gave me freedom from the opinion of what others might think. He gave me beauty for ashes and a right and sound mind through Christ. When life is not perfect, He still gives me His perfect presence and His perfect answer. In your life and mine, His answer may not always feel like the perfect word for the moment, but we can trust Him and give it time.

God Is Extraordinary

There was a time when Steve's company decided to move us to Dallas. We were just beginning to start the final finishing touches and landscaping on our second home on the other two-and-a-half acres that we owned in Fort Smith. This home was our dream home that we planned on living in forever. One morning while I was at Steve's office, I casually asked the president of the company if he could assure me that we would be staying in Fort Smith, because I didn't want to spend the extra money finishing our home if we weren't sure. He promised me we would be staying in Arkansas. We had barely settled into our newly completed home when the company that hired Steve to manage the large clinic in Fort Smith decided to relocate him so that he could oversee three larger clinics in Texas. With that decision, we had to move to Dallas—the very thing the president assured us would not happen!

I was shocked at the lack of integrity and devastated with the outcome, but regardless of my feelings, we moved to Dallas. We had just begun to make friends in Dallas when—*bam!* The company shut down overnight, and suddenly there we were in Dallas with nowhere to go and no job.

I was terrified. I was angry at the company and their failed promises. I was so bewildered that I couldn't sleep.

During one of those sleepless nights, instead of tossing and turning, I literally crawled out of bed and into our big walk-in closet, picking up my Bible that was lying on the floor on the way. In my closet, sitting on the floor, I began to read about the power we have been given over the Enemy—over serpents and scorpions and all things that sting your spirit and kill your soul. At the *very* minute I was reading about scorpions, a large scorpion came out of nowhere, walking toward me with its tail curled high. I was frozen with fear. I just sat there. I couldn't even move as it came closer and closer. When it got to me, I grabbed my Bible and slammed it down on that disgusting creature. As soon as I did that, I heard the Lord clearly speak, *"I still give you power to tread upon serpents and scorpions. I have not given you a spirit of fear, but of power and a sound mind."*

All fear left me immediately! I was mystified! I got up calmly and walked back to bed, thinking to myself, "Amazing! God will go to great lengths to make His convincing point!" He is not a God of fear; He despises its place in our lives.

When I walked into my closet the next morning, my Bible was still where I had slammed it down. Ever so carefully I picked it up, and there laid the evidence that not only the experience the night before had been real, but God's power was more real because I was peaceful, hopeful, and even happy!

If the Lord spoke to His people in the Old and New Testaments, why would He stop speaking in modern times? He is the Lord who is the same yesterday, today, and forever. He doesn't change—we do. He desires to have a relationship with us more than we can humanly comprehend.

I had been so entrapped in fear that my trust in God was bound by many what-ifs. I had more fear of Satan's swirling, relentless lies than faith in God's love and provision.

God Breaks Paradigms

The Bible tells us the story of a young boy named Samuel who was taken to the tabernacle to serve the high priest. While he was there, he heard God call his name in the middle of the night. The first two times Samuel heard God's call, he didn't know what to think, and he didn't recognize it as God's voice. Instead, he got up and went to Eli and said, "Here I am, for you called me."

The third time Samuel showed up that night, Eli recognized what was going on. He told Samuel to go back to his bed and when God spoke again, to say, "Speak, for your servant is listening" (1 Samuel 3:1–11 NIV).

Don't miss the profound truths in this story! You may not recognize that it is God speaking to you the first time you hear His voice. You might think, "That's just me thinking out loud." If the Lord spoke to His people in the Old and New Testaments, why would He stop speaking in modern times? He is the Lord who is the same yesterday, today, and forever. He doesn't change—we do. He desires to have a relationship with us more than we can humanly comprehend.

God Dislikes Boxes

God speaks to mankind in many different ways, and has since the beginning of time in the garden. Yet, we often question our hearing, thinking, "Oh, that can't be God. He's not like that. He wouldn't say something like that."

He is an infinite God, without beginning or end, who will be forever revealing Himself, yet we want to put Him in a box and label Him. You can be sure that just as soon as we think we know how things are or should be, He will break out of our manmade box and defy our limited thinking and small imaginations. My good friend Milt used to say, "He is God and He likes being God—can you blame Him?"

God is recorded in the Scriptures as speaking through angels; special messengers He sends from heaven with a specific message for a specific person.

God also speaks through ministers and speakers. If the words being spoken hit the core of your spirit, mind, or emotions, don't let them go—God is probably speaking to you.

God often speaks to us through songs or books. He speaks to our daughter Jessica during prayer and He speaks to Rebekah through worship. Think of the anointed books that have changed or eternally impacted your life. Do you believe you heard God speak to you through those pages?

God Speaks Directly to Our Spirit

The best response to hearing from God is to say, in essence, "I want to hear what you want to say to me. I want to know you. And, I want our relationship to be experientially real!" Some people have no desire to hear the Lord.

The effectiveness of God's Word is never in question—because He is love, we can trust His answers and His ways. We can trust what He is saying to us. I want to live as a person who is profoundly loved and cared for by a powerful, wise, and ever-present God. I want to live with peace, joy, and confidence.

> **It is God's nature to live out of His love, to heal, restore, and strengthen.**

I trust Him and I trust what He says. We cannot always trust our own thinking or nature, but His ways are so much higher and way outside our earthly boxes. Remember, He loves you, He loves me, and His plans for us and others are birthed out of His perfect love for our triumph on this earth.

God Has Answers and Solutions

For every challenge we encounter, God has a direction for us to walk, in order to get out of confusion and go into a new reality that is greater and more wonderful than what we left behind.

I do not want to mislead you into thinking that God's direction is always immediate or easy. The good news is that God has an amazing ability to break down seemingly impossible answers, solutions, and directives into small steps—both literal steps we can take and figurative steps in our thinking, planning, dreaming, and feeling. As we keep walking and trusting in Him, we are changed! Most of the time we are unaware of the transformation that has taken place.

Emotionally, I was not healed completely from the deep wounds of the tragedies I experienced in days, weeks, months, or even longer, but I know this: I did experience healing and transformation. It is God's nature to live out of His love, to heal, restore, and strengthen. God will always be true to His nature. He will always do in us and through us what will transform us into His image and equip us for our destiny on earth. He will always do His part. We can count on that even if we can't fathom how it might happen or what might be the result. Our part is to take His hand, walk by His side, and trust Him.

There are individuals and families who have suffered more than we have and there are those who have suffered less. On both sides, we wonder "How?" and "Why?" I don't have precise answers, but I have learned to trust that God loves me and He is a good Father who will take my hand and walk with me through all of the circumstances, good or bad.

The day that I lifted Andrew from Jessica's arms, I used lifesaving tactics that I had learned during my time as a lifeguard many years earlier. I knew the basics. In the same way, I believe the Lord calls each of us to learn the basics about how to receive and give His love, His forgiveness, and His mercy. Just as I breathed my breath into Andrew's lungs, we must learn how to breathe God's breath into desperate individuals and situations.

When I look back at my life, I sometimes say, "How did I get through? How did my marriage survive? How did my two wonderful daughters come forth whole and loving God more today than yesterday?" I know the answers lie in our responding to God's call to trust Him and receive His great love and grace. He was a first responder to each of us in our specific, great need. He was and still is more than sufficient for all of our greatest needs.

God Is Patient

I did not learn to discern the voice of God overnight—it has taken years of walking with Him by faith to learn how to recognize His voice. I do not hear Him perfectly all the time because I am still human; however, though my natural hearing is failing, my spiritual hearing is getting much stronger!

Recognizing the voice of God is a learning experience and usually begins with a desire or a need.

There is a generation arising that is full of people who seek answers and direction for their lives from *other* spiritual sources. Look at many of the movies—they are filled with the supernatural, both good and evil.

"In the beginning, God . . . " He is the original supernatural source. Satan came after God, yet the world seems to recognize his power and presence readily. That is strange to me.

Recognizing the voice of God is a learning experience and usually begins with a desire or a need. A baby has to learn to recognize the sound of a voice, usually that of their mother, father, or sibling. It begins as a need, and then hopefully, becomes a desire—a word or two here and there, then a sentence, and finally a full conversation.

I have misheard or misunderstood what the Lord was saying—a lot. But, it has always been in my heart to know the Holy Spirit better and to hear Him more clearly.

Words for Reflection

"Then you will call on me and come and pray to me, and I will listen to you. You will seek me and find me when you seek me with all your heart" (Jeremiah 29:12–13 NIV).

Hearing God's voice can be as simple as asking Him your deepest questions in your most challenging times, then listening with your heart, mind, and ears to His faithful answers.

Remember, His answer or wisdom may not immediately align with your heart or mind, but if it is God speaking, His answer will eventually make sense, bring peace, and give direction.

If you want or need to hear from God, ask Him right now to speak to you. Then just be attentive for an answer or direction that may come immediately, or perhaps in moments that follow, or perhaps in the very near future.

13

Two Challenges:
Hearing, Then Agreeing

In learning to hear God's voice, I believe a person faces two main challenges. The first is trusting that God still speaks, and the second is letting peace lead your decisions. For me, I normally need to focus on being quiet and still in order to really hear Him. I do hear God, at times, while I'm on the run. I can hear Him sometimes when I pray for someone in a group where there may be distractions. But, I almost always hear the Lord within my being or through the Bible when I am still. Either way, His spoken and written words are never without power.

My first challenge is being able to receive the message that I think is from God. Sometimes, I stubbornly refuse to receive His message because it is simply not what I want to hear. *I am learning, still, not to filter His message through my own pain, conflicting attitudes, fear, and personal desires.*

When God told me that *waiting was a good thing*, it was something that I truly needed to hear, because until that moment I had never considered that possibility. Waiting helps minimize giants until our faith can rise up to take down our fear or lack of trust. I wanted an immediate solution to the problem I was facing and, of course, I wanted God to tell me what I wanted to hear. I wonder if waiting ever gets easy—it is still a difficult thing for me to do. My strong will and decisiveness are good character traits, but only when they are first yielded to God's purpose and time.

When God spoke to me about *turning water to wine*, I *thought* I knew how to interpret those words and apply them to our situation. Looking back, I didn't have a clue.

Then, the word from the Bible about *slaying me*. How does one process something like that without faith in a good God?

And, lastly, *looking beyond* what I saw when the obvious was so very clear.

However, the more I have yielded to the Lord through the years, the more I have felt empowered to trust God. If He truly watches over His own word to perform it in us, which He tells us He does, then what other better option do we have when faced with various situations, trials, or temptations?

Challenge One: Trust That God Still Speaks Today

I suspect that we hesitate between two opinions more than we like to admit. And why do we do this? Because we haven't yet learned to fully recognize *who* is speaking and to believe that He is really speaking to us. Perhaps we have trouble trusting ourselves and trusting Jesus.

> *Our thoughts can be a powerful stronghold of either good or evil. I always tell myself, "Stop! Think about what you are thinking."*

When I first activated the voice-recognition tool on my smart phone, I was asked to repeat three times, "Hey, Siri." Now Siri can recognize my voice and follow my commands. God had to do the same thing with me, although it took many more than three times, and sometimes today, "Hey, Judy" still does not get my attention.

The Enemy is very shrewd—he knows what we *want* to hear, and he knows the arguments that will have the greatest influence on us. He is cunning and speaks half-truths, saying just enough truth to trick us into agreeing.

Satan did not confront Eve by saying, "God didn't say what you think He said." Rather, he inserted just a little bit of doubt, asking Eve, "Did God really say that?"

Satan's first strategy is to get us to doubt God and then to blame or accuse. His second strategy is to twist ever so slightly the goodness and love of God, causing us to doubt God's love, wisdom, and direction. I remind others and myself, "Listen to what you are thinking!" Our thoughts can be a powerful stronghold of either good or evil. I always tell myself, "Stop! Think about what you are thinking." We often develop the habit of letting our thoughts run wild.

God did not cause Andrew to fall into our pool. What He did do was *pause* time, like He did for Joshua on the battlefield, so that Joshua could prevail over the enemy. God held off Andrew's imminent death so that Steve and I could have time to get ourselves together and receive the power of His presence and His word in order to make it through victoriously.

It truly is a miracle, in my opinion, that an eternal, supernatural God speaks to mortal, natural people. It is equally miraculous that we can recognize and understand what He says to us! Oh, how He loves us!

Just think about it: God's words must penetrate our screen of expectations, then filter through all of the traditions, opinions, and biases that we have accumulated since we were born, then move past our prejudices, doubts, and ego-focused desires for self-gratification. After all of that, once we have registered His words, they must be solidified in our memories so that the Holy Spirit can remind us of what God has said!

God's words are not from a natural or fallen state, where our words come from. He speaks to us to lift us out of that natural state of thinking and action. His words put us onto higher ground. That is powerful! And we need all the power we can get to walk victoriously on this earth.

We do not know how many times God said to Adam and Eve in the garden of Eden, "Don't eat of that tree—the one you know as the Tree of Knowledge of Good and Evil."

Even after being so clear, a cunning creature—a beautiful disguise for Lucifer himself—came to Eve one day and asked, "Did God really say what you think He said?" He cast doubt on God's character, asking, "Did He really mean what it sounds like He meant, or what you think He meant?" When seeds of doubt begin to sprout, they interfere with faith.

When God spoke to me in the hospital, I knew without a doubt the words were from God. I may not have fully understood what they meant, but the words I heard were followed by peace. But, right after God's words were imparted to my heart, the Enemy came with a counterargument, *"Did God really say that?* What does He really mean? Perhaps He was saying . . . " And seeds of doubt and confusion set in. The war is always over God's word, written or spoken, because no word of God is without power. Satan wants to strip us of our ability to stand by causing us to doubt what the Lord is saying or has said.

Without any doubt, God *is* a divine healer. I have witnessed unfathomable miracles. I have laid hands on many people and prayed for a miracle without witnessing or knowing the outcome, but I have also prayed for a few and seen a physical healing come to pass immediately. I have been given specific words or actions for people—some of whom I knew, some acquaintances, and some total strangers. With every word that has come forth from the Lord, I have witnessed physical and emotional healing. I have seen hope displace confusion and despair. I have seen that "aha moment" transform a face and a heart that says, "He really knows me and He cares." Hearing a supernatural and all-powerful voice speak such intimate details about or to someone is astounding and fun! God is a healer, but it is never Satan who chooses who, how, when, and where God heals.

> **"Let peace be your umpire."**
>
>

Challenge Two: Let God's Peace Be the Best Umpire

When I was a very young Christian, new in the Christian faith, I heard a wise man say, "Let peace be your umpire." He went on to say, "If peace remains for three days, you have hit a home run in your understanding. If not, then it is a strikeout. Satan cannot bring true peace, and certainly not lasting for three days." Wait on the Lord, and if it takes three days to get to peace, then it takes three days—just don't get off of the base until it comes.

God's purpose is for His kingdom to be established within us at the time of salvation. We are to bring His kingdom to earth—Jesus taught his disciples this when He taught them to pray what we now call "The Lord's Prayer": "Thy kingdom come . . . in earth, as it is in heaven." Jesus said that His kingdom is righteousness, peace, and joy in the Holy Spirit that is within us.

My salvation was a miracle, and it was accompanied by lasting peace and joy. I experienced the supernatural peace of God as it came and brought a perfect calm to my best childhood friend when seconds before she was wailing and out of control—that's a miracle. The resolute peace in my faith that Jessica's arm would be physically healed, defying medical science, is a miracle.

One day as Steve and I prayed for a young woman we knew who had been dismissed from the hospital with severe, debilitating scoliosis, we watched and heard the sound of her backbone as it came into alignment. That was more than five years ago. When I saw her again recently, I asked her how her back was. "Perfect. No pain and no more hospitalizations!" *She walks in peace and joy—spirit, soul and body!*

But, there's another big part of that story. Years before we prayed for her, she had a dream about an older couple who would pray for her, and she would be healed. The man had silver hair and the woman had brown hair. She looked for years for that couple, and she let peace be her umpire while she waited to find them. When we walked into her office and asked her if we could pray for her healing, she told us about her dream. We were her dream come true—like a fairy tale, except it really happened. That is faith. That is God!

There are other divine miracles that I have witnessed through prayer. I fully believe in the supernatural workings of a supernatural creator; I just can't say when or how—that's His arena. I can just pray, believing and trusting in the wisdom of Father God who is good. His methods not only produce miracles, they bring His kingdom within us and around us.

Satan wants to set up his argument in a way that defies our faith. A great scheme of his is to steal our peace, to steal our joy, and to cause us to question, making us the center of the equation. Satan did not make the battle for Andrew a tug-of-war between God and himself; he made the battle for Andrew's life a tug-of-war between God and me. He tried to cause me to doubt God's love for me. *Could I win against God? Would I speak against God if He didn't do it my way? Could I outdo God when it came to loving my precious son?*

Look for God's kingdom to be established in the midst of turmoil or tragedy. Righteousness, peace, and joy are the necessities on which faith can be fortified. Those who wait on the Lord will mount up like an eagle and they will soar above and not stumble over.

Words for Reflection (and Declaration)

"He will call upon Me, and I will answer him; I will be with him in trouble; I will rescue him and honor him" (Psalm 91:15 NASB).

"Peace I leave with you; my peace I give you. I do not give to you as the world gives. Do not let your hearts be troubled and do not be afraid" (John 14:27 NIV).

This verse has been a pillar for me for decades.

"Yet, those who wait for the Lord will gain new strength; they will mount up with wings like eagles, they will run and not get tired, they will walk and not become weary (Isaiah 40:31 NASB).

"Reflection" is thinking deeply about God's truth.

"Declaration" is declaring God's truth and putting it into action, even before you understand it clearly and your emotions are steady.

Step into the Quiet—Listen

Jesus said to those who heard Him preach and teach, "He who has ears to hear, let him hear!" (Matthew 11:15).

The implication here is that not everybody wants to hear. Those who have no desire to hear from God rarely do. Those who deeply desire to hear from God nearly always do. Some do not hear because they do not take time to wait and listen to what the Lord might have to say. They have not learned to hear by developing a quiet zone.

I believe that I have heard repeatedly from God throughout my life because I truly want and need to hear from Him. The times He has spoken to me outside of the Bible usually have a personal purpose that is for the moment.

A book that was very profound to me as a young Christian woman was *The Sacred Romance*. In it, the author wrote:

Satan is constantly at work deconstructing the Sacred Romance in our heart so that he may more easily seduce us to the smaller stories he is telling. His purpose is to convince us that we need to create a story to live in that is not as dangerous as the Sacred Romance. As long as we do not admit that the deep things of our heart are there— the rejection and hurt, the shame and sorrow, the anger and rage— these rooms in our heart become darkened and the enemy sets up shop there to accuse us.

I have found myself questioning repeatedly, although less often now, the Lord's ability to get through to this heart of mine. It is amazing to me that He can bypass my mental and emotional state, whether in peace or crisis, and have His message register to me in the moment.

My natural temptation is to move myself away from the deep longing to see God's whole kingdom come on earth, and to be okay with mediocrity, which I see as a form of safety, adopting the approach to blend in and avoid taking the hits (see Luke 4:18–19). Therein lies the seduction—being satisfied with the smaller stories about God and me, and about God and you.

It's natural to play it safe, and even play it religiously safe. As my dear friend Milt once said at a conference, "Why do we as Christians, sons and daughters of the most powerful Father God, have the mentality to just 'hang in there and let the rough end drag?'" In the natural world, most people find it easier to "hang in there," but I don't want to be natural. I want to be super-natural! So many people, young included, are enticed with the superheroes—their movies are so popular. God is looking for the person who will take the risks to be supernaturally different!

Jesus said, "Come to Me, all who are weary and burdened, and I will give you rest. Put My yoke upon your shoulders . . . Learn from Me, for I AM gentle and humble of heart. *When you are yoked to Me*, your weary souls will find rest. For My yoke is easy and My burden is light" (Matthew 11:28–30 Voice). This is one of my favorite Bible verses—it is a promise from Jesus that I have found to be absolutely true and prevailing.

This verse is meaty—He says, "Come unto Me." Jesus will give you rest for your body, mind, will, and emotions. Oh, the war of worry that goes on in our stressed bodies and tormented emotions and mind, but Jesus is the Prince of Peace.

I have learned how to discipline myself to get quiet and listen. I have learned how to step out of the storm and into the safe room, a place of prayer. I have forced myself to quit running off half-cocked, with a partial message or word. I have learned to discard the other voices of well-meaning friends and acquaintances. I have taken the authority given to me through Christ and silenced the voices of the demonic realm that try to flood my mind and emotions with what-if and if-only ideas and with blame and accusation—two of the Devil's greatest tactics targeted at us but primarily at the Lord.

With tragedies or despairing difficulties, days can turn into weeks and weeks into months before the realization comes that the sorrow has lifted, the voice of Satan has diminished, and the Prince of Peace has regained His rightful throne in my heart. Unwavering peace is a true sign of healing. The battle has not only been won, but also resolved—I will not die, but live a full and productive life without fear, and I will declare the goodness and steadfastness of the Lord.

Am I more attentive to any unattended small child in or near a pool? Yes, but I am motivated by wisdom not fear.

When Steve lifted up little Andrew's lifeless body to the Lord in that sacred hospital room, we all declared our love, devotion, faith, and trust in the resurrected Lord. This *giving up* of Andrew was part of our receiving a greater trust in the Lord. Once a surrendering sacrifice is offered, it cannot be taken back. Our sacrifice was our absolute trust and surrender to the Lord's amazing goodness and grace.

So far, I have learned a lot from life and its experiences. The brilliant plan of the Lord is that He gives me the privilege to learn. It's not that I have to do anything, but that I get to do a lot of things.

Shush! God Is Speaking

The phrase "spiritual ears" refers to a person's God-given ability to hear what God means through their spirit. God's messages are always grounded in the context of eternity. When He speaks to us, He is speaking a message that was true in eternity past, is true in the present, and will be true in eternity future.

Our natural ears let us perceive and take in sounds made on this earth, but they are limited to a particular spectrum of hearing and to a wide variety of conditions that can alter our ability to perceive correctly or understand completely. We also tend to interpret words or sounds on the basis of our current feelings. People in shock or deep grief, for example, can hear the same words as a person sitting next to them who is *not* in shock or grief, and come away with a much different understanding about what was said and what it meant.

Spiritual ears allow us to hear in a way that gets as close to the *why* or *how* answers to life's experiences as possible. *Spiritual hearing is hearing from God's perspective.* The words of God do not lose power over time and they are not easily forgotten. I remember them (like you've read in this book)—they are part of my testimony, and the Bible says that we overcome by the blood of the Lamb *and* the word of our testimony. My testimonies are not hearsay—I was there for it all.

We may never fully have an answer to why—to this day, we don't know exactly *why* God allowed Andrew to live on this earth for only eighteen months before taking him into eternity. But I can tell you explicitly what the Lord revealed to me in the hospital and how it has affected my life. God's word has eternal power, whether it is written in the Bible or spoken to one's spirit.

For example, I heard the Lord clearly say, **"Waiting is not a bad thing,"** yet, I still have trouble *waiting*. As an adult, I struggle with waiting because so much can be accomplished out of my own will and strength, but the reward just doesn't have the lasting impact and satisfaction that comes when I wait on the Lord. Isaiah recorded, "Those who wait for the Lord will gain new strength; they will mount up with wings like eagles; they will run and not get tired, they will walk and not become weary." Therefore, that truth alone tells me that waiting is a good thing, or as I heard from the Lord, **"Waiting is not a bad thing . . . *Judy!*"** (my emphasis).

The Lord also said to me, ***"Your water will be changed into wine."*** *That is transformation.* Looking back, I have seen changes in myself that I did not notice at first because they took place over time. These are some of the changes:

- ◆ *My perspective has shifted*—I now want to care more about what God knows and thinks about me rather than what others think about me. I do not want the concern of people and their opinion to dominate my thoughts and actions, so I try to evaluate situations from a higher vantage point, even if it's unpopular.

- ◆ *"The schedule"* doesn't have dictating power over me anymore—it's all about what you get to do rather than what you have to do. I realize I truly have a *choice* in how to spend my time, not just because I am older and do not have that much to do. In fact, I can find myself busier and more called upon than when I was in my twenties and thirties, but I have learned how to say, "No," without explanation or excuses.

- ◆ I would rather have fun than be pretentious or worried about what others might think.

◆ I have experienced eternal values that are much more rewarding and satisfying than the temporal choices I used to make much more frequently.

Recently, Steve and I were facing a huge financial crisis in which everything we owned was threatened. I remembered those words spoken to me in a hospital long ago, "Look beyond what you see," and yet here I was feeling panicked. I cried, I prayed, and I railed against our situation, but all I could see was the doom and the loss of everything. Why couldn't I see beyond the devastation this time?

> *"Stand still and see the salvation of the Lord." Not only did I hear Him speak, but immediately, I felt His presence and peace envelop me.*

It was in the midst of desperate prayer that I heard the Lord's quiet voice say, *"Stand still and see the salvation of the Lord."* Not only did I hear Him speak, but *immediately*, I felt His presence and peace envelop me. It felt so surreal, yet His voice was very real. He just doesn't give up on us. I settled down and began to focus beyond what I saw and how I felt. I focused on His goodness and His faithfulness. I sensed His power shoring me up and returning hope. Within a week, a magnificent financial deliverance came to us from an anonymous source and brought us out of the pending doom of bankruptcy and loss. We need willingness and grace to listen to the voice that matters most. When you seem to be flailing, that is the time to be still, wait, and trust. Really, what else is there to do? Except, perhaps, panic and then grow bitter and unbelieving.

I have witnessed physical and emotional changes occur when I have prayed God's Word over someone. His Word is living—like a two-edged sword—it divides one's belief from disbelief and allows faith to have its way.

While the miracle of Jesus turning water into wine at the wedding at Cana happened in just minutes, I am okay that God is transforming me over time. The evidence of transformation is seen and experienced, just as the wine at the wedding was changed, seen, and experienced. My transformation process started when I asked Jesus to be my Savior—I might be becoming a fine wine!

I know that God speaks through impressions, creations, visions, dreams, prophecies, prayers, songs, and in a "still, small voice." We are wise to practice listening. When we listen, we actually can hear! My questions to myself and others are, "Do we really want or care to hear what God is saying? Are our lives too busy or frantic to take time to hear His still, small voice?"

I believe that God speaks primarily through His Word; however, in the midst of the financial wave that was crashing on us, I heard the Lord say in my spirit, ***"Stand still and see the salvation of the Lord."*** Later, I realized the words I heard above were a directive found in Exodus 14:13. *I heard Him speak to me, and then days later, I found it in the Bible.* His written Word has been given to us precisely for that purpose, to know Him and what He is like through the accounts of men and women who witnessed His life on the earth.

> *A wonderful pastor whom I deeply admire once said, "I read until I hear my own voice in the Scripture."*

I understand that! I believe it is truly a miracle that the Word of God infuses us and empowers us. My good words to others will never have the power to heal and change like the Word of God.

In my opinion and experience, the best place to start is with the Bible or daily devotionals. Our mentors, long ago, encouraged us to read *My Utmost for His Highest* by Oswald Chambers. I still read it today—it's such a quick way to start your day. It's hard to argue with the Word of God if you believe He exists, if you believe He is all-wisdom, if you believe He is all-love, and especially if you are a believer in Jesus Christ. The Bible is the Holy Spirit's written love letter to us.

> *Transformation is God's plan to turn us from ordinary people into extraordinary people who are filled to the brim and overflowing with the supernatural presence of God.*

Press in Closer, You Can Hear Better

We also are able to hear God speaking to us through the Holy Spirit within us and through modern-day prophets, preachers, and pastors. There is not a superior form— the only difference is that the written Word of God, the Bible, is more readily available to us.

How does anybody take in all that God desires to say on any subject after just one reading in the Bible? There are so many levels of meaning and depths of wisdom—remember, God is infinite and forever revealing Himself to us!

Transformation is God's plan to turn us from ordinary people into extraordinary people who are filled to the brim and overflowing with the supernatural presence of God. People who have been transformed through salvation can actually hear God speak through the Bible and through young and old people because they are able to recognize a holy voice that is not their own. People do amazing things that have lasting results because they have developed a place for the Lord's word, whether written or spoken.

Words for Reflection

"Your ears shall hear a word behind you, saying 'This is the way, walk in it,' whenever you turn to the right hand or whenever you turn to the left" (Isaiah 30:21).

Often, we must listen to God's guidance as we go to hear His confirmation or re-direction. What is God saying to you in your journey as you travel your course?

Waiting Is Not a Bad Thing

When I first heard the Lord say to me in the hospital that "waiting is not a bad thing," my first reaction was, *"How can it be a good thing?"*

I argued with the Lord, pleading for Him to act instantly on Andrew's behalf. He didn't. I realized later that even if the Lord had said, "I'm going to do this exact miracle that you want in the next ten minutes," that ten-minute wait would have seemed excruciatingly long to me in my hour of crisis, and I probably still would have said, "Go faster, God!"

I certainly did not comprehend the full meaning or consequence of God's words to me. I still have trouble associated with waiting, but learning is like that, isn't it? We learn at one level and then we are taken to another level of learning to encounter additional lessons. With each lesson comes added information, greater understanding, and increased wisdom. The learning never really ends in this lifetime.

So, while I still don't fully understand how waiting can be a good thing—or at least not a bad thing—I do know this:

Waiting on the Lord is a good thing because His wisdom and guidance and the answers that are revealed during the

> *Waiting on the Lord is a good thing because His wisdom and guidance and the answers that are revealed during the waiting period flow from the goodness of His heart.*
>
>

waiting period flow from the goodness of His heart. The waiting time is truly the cocoon that is protecting your heart until your will is yielded to the Lord's truest and highest goodness. This cocoon surrounds you against the outside environment of suppositions, doubts, and fears. Waiting on the Lord is also a guard against self-sufficiency and pride. As we Texans say, "Just pull yourself up by your bootstraps," but sometimes those bootstraps break. Lessons related to waiting have been the most difficult for me.

I see in such black-and-white terms, but waiting gives the gray area a chance to clarify. Waiting is like a fog to me—it forces me to slow down and let time be my friend until God's purpose, plan, or words become clear.

I know God is perfect and He is perfect in loving me and guiding me—He is my Savior. In the anxious moments, however, I tend to believe I know what is best for me and I convince myself that I can handle the situation or crisis. In waiting, suddenly there's that cocoon of love, softly shielding me from myself and my human reasoning. God is my Father and He created me; therefore, He has an answer for every question and every dilemma, and He has perfect timing in speaking to me.

The problem then becomes me being unruly when I have to wait, but as I emerge from the waiting cocoon, I see much more clearly—mostly I see Him *high and lifted up.* I see that He is God and that He really does love me and has kind and good plans for me. I cannot see my future or anyone else's! That is why we must learn the art of waiting in peace and absolute trust.

Even so, there is nothing easy about waiting. There's nothing about waiting that feels like a good idea to me and there's nothing about waiting that I enjoy. Nevertheless, I am learning to wait on the Lord and His promises. Waiting protects me from getting ahead of Him, so that I can walk with Him while holding His hand, and because it is what God said is good for me!

What Happens During a Waiting Time?

◆ Waiting gives us the time we need to refocus our eyes from the darkness so we can take in the light. It gives us time to see, hear, and understand things from God's perspective.

◆ Waiting gives us an opportunity to rekindle our faith and trust.

◆ Waiting gives us time to reconnect our heart to God's heart and change our thinking.

In our waiting, as we depend on the Lord these things happen:

◆ Character grows within us . . . silently but persistently. The Spirit does His work in growing the fruit within us that reflects the nature of Christ Jesus.

◆ Courage has time to take root and grow.

◆ Gratefulness begins to invade our speech.

◆ Wisdom begins to germinate, sprout, and produce visible manifestations.

◆ Faith, which is believing that God exists, begins to grow into genuine trust, which is believing that God can and will manifest His presence and power in the very best way for us. Trust becomes the foundation for truly accepting that God is always in control. "Que será, será" may be a good song sung by Doris Day, but it's just not true in God's world.

God's great purposes in waiting are that we might grow into a greater, unshakeable trust and understand more and more of God's heart and purposes. Growth is not instantaneous. It takes time, and ultimately, it requires our willingness to participate in the process. He will even wait on you. He will not cross your will. *Your will activates your faith and trust, which enables you to be empowered to wait upon the Lord.*

Two Sides to Waiting

Again, it's like in Joni Mitchell's song about clouds—the sun is shining above the clouds, but from earth's perspective, we only see the dark underside until the sun breaks through.

I like to think of waiting as having a light side and a dark side. The light side might be called "joyful anticipation." Think about Christmas—waiting skills are challenging, particularly for small children when they're in the presence of fancy baubles and glimmering lights on trees that normally aren't in the house. Brightly wrapped packages invite them to take just one peek.

Many years ago, when I was a child, my younger brother and I awoke very early one Christmas morning, and we grew tired of waiting for the rest of the family to wake up. So we sneaked into our dark living room with the intention of opening just one little gift each. That, of course, led to two gifts and then to three. You can guess the rest of the story. Our parents and older brothers were very disappointed at what we had done, but their disappointment wasn't anything compared to our feelings of guilt and sadness. We had ruined the thrill of a family Christmas celebration.

This *light* kind of waiting is upbeat and exciting, but it is still hard to do. Even this kind of waiting—with a very high likelihood that the outcome will be joyful—requires a strength of self-restraint and calls us to the wisdom of timing.

The *dark* kind of waiting is not as upbeat—we don't see everything so clearly and beautifully. It is more intense and intentional. It is rarely spontaneous or sporadic. It is like the athlete who prepares for years to compete in just one event. The years of waiting and training for the right time and the right event, again, require a strength of self-restraint and the wisdom of timing.

We often find that how excruciating it feels to wait is directly proportional to how badly we want a specific outcome, especially when that outcome isn't guaranteed. The waiting becomes even more excruciating in situations where there is no sure outcome. We may not believe that God has heard our prayers, much less that He will answer them in the way that we desire. Waiting in these instances is unavoidable, but it gives us an opportunity to grow in discernment and in our belief of God's faithfulness.

This is when we should rehearse our lines, "God is good. God is merciful. God loves me more than I love myself. I can trust God because He is for me. He will cause me to soar like an eagle over the earthly concern. God's grace is sufficient for all my needs—even if I don't feel it. God will never leave me, forsake me, or lie to me. I can really trust God! Steady me, God! I need you and every benefit you have for me. God, you are my helper, kind and good, help me!"

What are you waiting for?

Are you waiting for the person of your dreams?
Are you waiting to see if your relationship will be reconciled?
Are you waiting for a baby?
Are you waiting for your child's marriage to be healed?
Are you waiting for your child's business opportunity to come through?

Are you waiting for a new opportunity, new income, or new position?

Are you waiting for a diagnosis?

Are you waiting for a failing business to turn around?

Are you waiting for a lost investment to be restored?

Are you waiting for a loan approval for your dream house or business?

Are you waiting for your child's broken heart to be healed?

Are you waiting for an answer to your heart's question?

Are you waiting for God's answer to you?

Waiting is not an easy thing to do, no matter how small or big or complicated the situation. The process is difficult, but it does have an ending. The process will reveal your strength, your future, and your hope. And when all is said and done, the goodness of God will become evident to you.

Making the Wait Easier

Focus on God's Goodness. I believe that the main thing that helps us wait is a new awareness of, or insight into, God's invincible and infinite goodness. So often we find it difficult to wait because we question whether we will end up with what we desire. We wonder if God might have forgotten the little stuff in lieu of the big stuff.

God's goodness stands in sharp contrast to human selfishness, shortsightedness, and feelings of desperation that we must make our lives happen on our own schedule in order to have any sense of progress or success. These feelings refute God's generosity, His ability to see far into the future, and His power to exert absolute control over all of His creation at all times.

Perhaps more than any other person in the Old Testament, Moses had a very strong understanding of God's goodness. *He saw God's goodness as God's glory.* When we speak about the glory of the Lord, we are actually referring to the radiant perfection of God's goodness—a goodness replete with love, mercy, and patience beyond measure. All aspects of beauty, harmony, and vibrancy are embodied in the goodness of God.

Focus on Times and Seasons. Decades ago, a popular song was written about this. The lyrics were based on a passage from the book of Ecclesiastes that describes the ebb and flow of life:

To every thing there is a season, and a time to every purpose under heaven:

A time to be born, and a time to die; a time to plant, and a time to pluck up that which is planted;

A time to kill, and a time to heal; a time to break down, and a time to build up;

A time to weep, and a time to laugh; a time to mourn, and a time to dance;

A time to cast away stones, and a time to gather stones together; a time to embrace, and a time to refrain from embracing;

A time to get, and a time to lose; a time to keep, and a time to cast away;

A time to rend, and a time to sew; a time to keep silence, and a time to speak;

A time to love, and a time to hate; a time of war, and a time of peace (Ecclesiastes 3:1–8 KJV).

> **"God doesn't spin us around to make us dizzy. He shows us Himself in the opposite dimensions of any experience, to reveal to us that He is always there for us."**

As a friend once said about this chapter in Ecclesiastes, "God doesn't spin us around to make us dizzy. He shows us Himself in the opposite dimensions of any experience, to reveal to us that He is always there for us."

If we are sad, He is joy. If we are hopeless, He is hope. If we are poor, He is rich. If we are broken, He is the fixer. If we see death, He reveals life. He helps us endure the negatives so that we can expand the positives, which then prepare us to take on the next round of negatives.

From a spiritual standpoint, of course, we are not caught in the ebb and flow of these states—they form more of a spiral than a fixed circle. It is only as we fully experience one dimension of a circumstance that we find that it prepares us for future dimensions!

God's purpose is not to keep us spinning in circles, but rather, to take us from height to height and glory to glory. He uses the common experiences of life—which are common to all people in all cultures and through all ages—

to challenge us, make us, mold us, refine us, and help us stop spinning in endless circles.

He is seeking to take us to a new, upward dimension of transformation that is going to result in a new level of fulfillment for our lives, and a greater opportunity for us to witness to others. He never leaves us where we are. He has a plan and purpose for us that is much higher than our present . . . He is bringing His kingdom on earth to us and through us, while preparing us for eternity!

We certainly don't like to think that there will be future negativity in our lives, especially if we have just been through a very painful and exhausting time, but just as surely as the sun will rise tomorrow, the sun will also set tomorrow night. The good will come, even if we cannot imagine it during our grieving or our sense of loss. And the same principle is at work about future challenges—perhaps the best possible outcome is that next time we will be a little stronger, a little wiser, and a little more resilient. God desires to take us from strength to strength.

And the best news of all, of course, is that one day—that glorious day when we leave earth behind and enter eternity—we will have no more earth-bound lessons to learn or circumstances to wrangle. We will only know the fullness of God's presence as He wraps His everlasting arms around us, and we will know only good things!

"He has made everything beautiful in its time. Also He has put eternity in their hearts . . . I know that whatever God does, it shall be forever. Nothing can be added to it, and nothing taken from it" (Ecclesiastes 3:11,14).

Try to See Time as God Sees It. God regards time differently than human beings do. He lives outside of time because there is no beginning or ending with Him—He is infinite! He remains above the clouds, until the light breaks through. He is the Light and He always breaks through. We can trust, and we need to trust, His timing and His way.

It is difficult for me, and I believe this to be true for most people, to fathom the truth that God has no beginning or ending, therefore my understanding of timing about when things should begin and end—ideally, opportunistically, or appropriately—is always going to be subject to my human desire and limited understanding.

Try to Focus beyond the Waiting Time. Waiting is all about time, and time is unpredictable and out of our control. Have you ever had to wait in an emergency room on a Saturday night? My friend and I did just that. While we were there, we focused on all of the bizarre things we saw and the myriad of attendants who checked on us and didn't do one thing about the dog-bite wound on my forehead. Even through the struggle, what we experienced made us laugh. Focus on the positive things—they are always there. Dark clouds have silver linings, you just have to look for them.

Jesus waited for eons at the doorway of heaven, watching millennia go by while people fell deeper and deeper into anger, bitterness, hatred, rebellion, and rejection of God the Father. He waited with a breaking heart as thousands and thousands of sacrificial lambs died on the altars of the tabernacle, and later the temple, to secure temporary moments of peace and relief from guilt and sin's stains. He just waited for the sound of the Father's voice to simply say, "Go. Now."

God the Father had waited until the "fullness of time," and when that moment arrived, love could no longer be restrained. God sent His only Son into the broken world to bring the means of reconciliation that would change eternal destiny for all who received God's plan.

While Jesus waited in His humanity, the Word of God says that He grew in wisdom and stature and understanding. He continued to manifest patience as He waited for the day when He would be the full embodiment of God's grace. That embodiment of grace required Him to *die* so that all mankind might have the opportunity to *live* eternally.

As our family waited for Andrew to wake up on earth, the Lord was preparing him to wake up in heaven in the full embodiment of God's grace.

In waiting, we discover the reality that we need hope and that Jesus' love is the only thing that gives us a future and hope. We can be assured that as we trust Him with our will yielded to His will, love and hope become ours. And when all else seems to fail, hope points to the Eternal One, the holy Three in One, and we again encounter His love and His desire to give us hope for our future. Sometimes eternal truths have to be revealed to us over and over, but the Lord is patient to wait for us as we wait on Him, and then we are empowered and can say, "Not my will, Lord, but your will be done—in me, to me, and through me." My yielded will brings me into the safe place of His grace and only then am I able to truly say, "I trust you."

Words for Reflection

"Wait on the Lord; be of good courage, and He shall strengthen your heart; wait, I say, on the Lord!" (Psalm 27:14).

Waiting is a source of inner strength that God shall grant to those who wait!

"Therefore I will look to the Lord; I will wait for the God of my salvation; My God will hear me" (Micah 7:7).

"Be still, my soul," says the famous hymn. The key to stillness is letting go of what-if and if-only.

"Have you not known? Have you not heard? The everlasting God, the Lord, the Creator of the ends of the earth, neither faints nor is weary. His understanding is unsearchable. He gives power to the weak, and to those who have no might He increases strength. Even the youths shall faint and be weary, and the young men shall utterly fall, but those who wait on the Lord shall renew their strength; they shall mount up with wings like eagles, they shall run and not be weary, they shall walk and not faint" (Isaiah 40:28–32).

This is one of the most powerful promises that should encourage any of us who are in a position of having to wait.

As we wait, we begin to separate from anger and worry. Oftentimes, fear is the root of these two deadly emotions. They are here only to harm us, and they never make the waiting process easier or shorter.

16

Fine Wine Takes Time

When the Lord spoke to me for the second time while we were in the hospital, saying, *"**Your water will be changed into wine**,"* I had a lot of questions and a lot of misinterpretations. I took the Lord's words to mean initially that Andrew's lifeless body—his physical shell—was going to be reinvigorated and transformed from lifeless to life filled!

It took me months to fully grasp that the *turning of water into wine* was the Lord talking about *my life*, not Andrew's. Unlike the water-to-wine miracle that happened in moments, transformation in a person's life is never finished on this earth.

Think about the miracle of Jesus turning water into wine at the wedding feast—it was Jesus' first public miracle and one that still holds tremendous intrigue (see John 2:1–11).

Wedding feasts in those days and in that part of the world were weeklong events. The ceremony was followed by feasting, merriment, dancing, music, and a lot of good food and wine. It was a once-in-a-lifetime celebration for the newly married couple, intended to be a time of supreme joy.

Jesus and members of His family were there. The moment came when the wine that had been purchased for the festivities ran out, which was a major social error! Jesus' mother came to Him and explained the problem, and Jesus knew she was expecting Him to solve the problem. Mary likely thought this would be done in a rather normal way; perhaps Jesus would send somebody with money to purchase more wine. Nobody expected Jesus to do what He did.

Jesus told the servants to fill the water jugs to the brim—these were twenty-gallon containers that were used for ceremonial washing before meals. The servants did as He instructed, and then Jesus told the servants to fill pitchers from the jugs that would be used to pour into the goblets of those at the feast. As the servants did this, they found that the water in the jugs had been *transformed* into the best wine that they had ever tasted. And that was in the opinion of the host of the wedding feast!

At last, the party could continue without any embarrassment to the newly married couple or their family members. The joy could flow freely!

This was not just a nice thing for Jesus to do, it was a demonstrated word of the Lord Jesus that had a distinctly prophetic edge to it! *Everything* that Jesus did—every word He spoke, every miracle He performed, every demonstration of mercy and love that He manifested—was going to be an act of transformation.

Those who had their sins forgiven by Jesus were transformed into a newness of spiritual life.

Those who were delivered from demons were transformed into a new dimension of living.

Those who were healed physically were transformed into a new life of service and work.

The turning of water into wine at a wedding in a small town in northern Galilee was a powerful and prophetic miracle that foretold the ultimate ministry of Jesus throughout eternity—everything Jesus does in the life of a human being is directed toward transformation!

> *This supernatural catch transformed their understanding about Jesus.*
>
>

Transformation leads to a new level of provision, or perhaps stated even better, *sufficiency*. The grace poured out in a time of need is sufficient to get the person to the other side of the need and into the answer or solution. His grace is our sufficiency.

We see it again and again in the miracles of Jesus.

On one occasion Jesus told a group of fishermen, who had loaned Him a boat as a preaching platform just offshore from a large crowd, to launch out into the water and cast their nets. The fishing in the Sea of Galilee normally took place at night, while this word of Jesus was probably made around midday or late afternoon. The owners of the boat were reluctant, but they obeyed, and they experienced what many have described as a "net-breaking" and "boat-sinking" load—so great a haul of fish that the boat owner had to call companion fishermen to help reel in the catch.

This supernatural catch not only fed those fishermen and their families for weeks and maybe even longer, but it also transformed their understanding about Jesus. Their lives were changed dramatically and completely in one hour of fishing!

Do not overlook the sufficiency that Jesus gave them—the generosity of His miracle was overwhelming and stunning.

As my darling baby boy lay in his hospital bed, I believed that God was about to do an amazing miracle beyond anything I could imagine, and that it would be a miracle of transformation both for Andrew and for me.

Certainly, I wanted there to be a miracle, but my idea was that the miracle would be a tremendous surge of healing power that would cause new life to fill Andrew so that he could come home with us. God, however, was getting ready to do an even greater miracle of transformation in Andrew's life, my life, and the lives of all who experienced his life and death along with us.

In many ways, Andrew had been depleted of his old life—his original allotment of joy, creativity, hugs, kisses, and squeals of laughter. In place of his old life, God was about to bring Andrew into a new life beyond the thin line that separates time and eternity. Andrew was just days away from being transformed into a life fit for the heaven in which he would find himself for all of eternity. He would have new health and energy beyond all bounds, and it would never end. He would discover countless things to enjoy, and he would experience new depths of creativity, wonderment, and fulfillment. He was on the brink of a new life that cannot be contained in any person's vocabulary, much less their thoughts; a new life that takes place in an atmosphere without even a wisp of evil or the slightest taint of sorrow.

> **The transformative work of Jesus Christ, through the Holy Spirit, begins the moment we accept Jesus as our Savior.**
>
>

Andrew was about to enter a new life marked by perpetual light, with colors, shapes, and perhaps even creatures of beauty beyond anything we know on earth—a little boy's wildest and most fun adventure—surrounded by total love and a depth of well-being that cannot be described.

He was about to be infused with a new mind that required a new spiritual body that would enable him to move, sense, and *know* the goodness and greatness of an almighty God in a way that he never had experienced during his time on earth and never would have been able to experience on earth.

Transformation! I cannot truly fathom the fact that our child was made completely new, fully resurrected to eternal life and all of its limitless splendor, in one heartbeat.

However, transformation can still begin now for all of us who remain on earth! The transformative work of Jesus Christ, through the Holy Spirit, begins the moment we accept Jesus as our Savior. When we invite Jesus to be our Savior, we simultaneously receive the presence of the Holy Spirit that Jesus promised to those who believe in Him.

Our proof that the process is working is that we begin to have new attitudes. Temporal values do not seem to have the power over us as they did before. We simply don't see other people the same way we once did. We don't relate to the stresses and pressures of life the way we used to. We now have little insights into *how* to be more like Jesus, and *what* to say and do in situations that once might have overwhelmed us. The bottom line is that love and forgiveness are realized by us and others.

"For it is God who works in you both to will and to do for His good pleasure" (Philippians 2:13).

It is a transformative work that brings us to the place where we really want to do God's will, and to do what God defines as His good pleasure. This is when we truly verge on moving fully into a life that brings heaven to earth—" . . . Thy kingdom come . . . on earth as it is in heaven!"

Transformation Is an Exchange Process

We exchange these:

◆ the darkness of our lives for His light

◆ our spiritual poverty for His spiritual riches

◆ our unforgiving heart for His forgiving one

◆ our weakness and hesitancy for His vibrancy and courage

◆ our limited understanding about life for His unlimited wisdom

◆ our failures for His victories

◆ our tragedies for His triumphs

◆ our lack for His sustenance

◆ our sorrow for His joy

There simply is no area of life that is not subject to His transformative power.

Transformation by God Is Marked by Joy!

Since transformation is linked to the concept of "new wine in new wineskins," which is *a concept also linked to joy,* there can be no doubt that God is quite adamant about us possessing joy. He wants our lives to be *full of joy and the reflection of joy.* He wants us to serve Him with joy and enter into the fullness of His joy.

He intends for His joy to remain as a fixed trait in our lives. Let me just say, joy is not a feeling or an emotion—it is a character trait and a quality of life to be possessed. In times of suffering, He desires that I patiently endure with joy, and that I even "count it all joy" when I encounter various trials and troubles in my life (see James 1:2–8). These feel like hard, seemingly impossible commands from Jesus, but when I remember the cost of highly refined gold and its stunning reflective beauty, I soften and yield to Him because I know that He will watch over me as He watches over His Word to perform it in me.

As impossible and unreasonable as it seems, I have been given a helper to guide me. He is the Holy Spirit. Fiery trials are very hard and sometimes don't seem possible, and they feel even more impossible when it comes to the command of counting it all joy. God promises if I will just do what He asks and trust Him, this fiery trial will have its perfect result in me, and I will be lacking in nothing.

The heavenly Father has proven to me over and over again that I can trust Him. He desires that I choose joy, but it is still my choice. My life today is not worse, it is better because I chose to count it all joy, as weak and helpless as I might have felt. I have so much more love, compassion, mercy, understanding, wisdom, truth, and joy in my older age. What I don't have is anger, sorrow, and jealousy. I have the proof that if I choose to count it all joy, the outcome may not be exactly as I predicted or desired, but the outcome will not have the power of bitterness within me.

Refining gold involves removing the impurities after the smelting process. Pure gold tends to be too soft for practical use, so it needs other metals to be added to it. Think about that further—as precious as it is, pure gold is too soft. It's interesting to compare that to the Lord's goal of refining—He wants us to be soft, teachable, and stunningly beautiful.

In 1 Peter 1:7, the Bible says that the proof of our faith, being more precious than gold, is tested (refined) by fire. How much greater is our value when we go through fiery trials and come through shining brightly on the other side?

Transformation Is a Process

In so many ways, transformation is the process that takes us from what *was* in our life to what *can* be . . . and beyond that, it takes us to what *will* be.

There are many examples in the natural world that show us God's transformation processes. A small, crawling creature that we call a caterpillar spins a cocoon around itself and appears dead to the world, and then one day, breaks out of that cocoon as a lovely butterfly that is capable of soaring away, no longer limited to crawling.

We see children grow up against seemingly impossible odds, learning, developing, and growing, to one day become adults who are capable of teaching and serving others in profound ways.

We see hardened hearts and stubborn wills softened to become loving hearts and flexible vessels capable of giving genuine love to others.

There is a part that we must do, but there is an even greater part that we must be willing to let God do in us and for us.

Genuine transformation cannot be self-engineered—it is always subject to processes set in time. Don't get frustrated with others and with yourself but be glad that *time* is in the Lord's hands.

Transformation Aspects

There are several aspects of transformation that I believe are wise for us to consider:

Take in Truth. First, we need to be willing to take truth into our minds. For me, the ultimate source of truth, and often the last source, is the Bible. The Bible says of itself that it has the power to renew and transform the thinking of our minds, and to liberate us from disbelief, doubts, and fears. The Bible refers to itself as the living Word of God. If we believe this is true, then it is relevant and personalized for each one of us.

Understand God's Desires. Second, we must ask the Lord to reveal to us an understanding of His desires for us. He tells us in His Word that He has a plan for us, our success, and our welfare. What are those plans and successes?

I have experienced and I am still experiencing these:

♦ *Genuine change.* We cannot help but change in various ways every day of our lives, but what we can do is ask the Lord to help us make choices that lead to positive change.

♦ *New perspective.* Time with the Bible and reasoning with God give us an ongoing new perspective about the way God sees our world. The Lord says, "Come, let us reason together." There are times I think that, just maybe, the Lord would rather I hadn't discovered that verse!

♦ *Empowerment.* It seems almost impossible on the surface to think that what we read in the Bible can strengthen us spiritually and emotionally, but the Bible says, "No Word of God is without power!" No Word!

> *His word, spoken or written, is like His own nature—it does not change even in the tiniest way, and yet, His word changes us in profound ways.*

The Bible says about itself that it is the "inspired" Word of God. The Holy Spirit who caused the truths of the Bible to be set into language and ink is the Holy Spirit who writes His love and truth on our hearts and lives. He takes what has been written, applies it to our lives today, and uses it to produce in us what will be our character, our desires, our messages, and our influence on the future.

His word, spoken or written, is like His own nature—it does not change even in the tiniest way, and yet, His word changes us in profound ways. His word compels growth, new thinking, and greater strength beyond anything we could imagine as a goal or plan. It changes what we desire, what we love, and what we think. The word of the Lord sharpens our perspective of ourselves and situations around us, and it produces life and hope in our human lives.

Look at What the Lord Has Done. I know that my transformation process on this earth is far from complete; however, it is encouraging for me to look back and see all that the Lord has done in me, for me, and even through me.

We are asked by God to be "looking unto Jesus, the author and finisher of our faith, who for the joy that was set before Him endured the cross" (Hebrews 12:2). It is His job to finish His work in me, and Jesus has promised to send the Holy Spirit to do at least these three things:

◆ reveal that Jesus is the author of our faith

◆ reveal that Jesus is the finisher, "completer," or "fulfiller" of our faith

◆ reveal that He is always present to help us endure the hardships of this life, even those directly linked to our very fulfillment as human beings, and to do so with joy

How do we go from glory to glory? How do we get better with age, like a fine wine? Transformation! It is a magnificent process.

The "cross" for us is anything that brings death to the dark ways of our self-nature. For me, I would consider pride and fear to be dark ways—they cloud the light of Christ's ways of humility and trust on earth.

But remember that beyond the cross is resurrection. Jesus knew what was beyond the cross for Himself. We, too, can know that beyond the severe suffering we experience is life again here on earth as well as in heaven.

Remember that the wedding at Cana was a most joyous occasion, but the outstanding thing that we remember from that event was when Jesus turned ordinary water into wine. The outcome of that miracle not only caused greater faith in His disciples, but it also allowed the joy of the event to continue! The joy became even greater joy!

How do we go from glory to glory? How do we get better with age, like a fine wine? Transformation! It is a magnificent process.

Words for Reflection

"And do not be conformed to this world, but be transformed by the renewing of your mind, so that you may prove what the will of God is, that which is good and acceptable and perfect" (Romans 12:2 NASB).

In Ephesians 4:13–15, we learn that the purpose of transformation is that we grow to maturity in Christ and into His measure of stature.

As believers, we are all being conformed and transformed into the nature and image of Jesus Christ—it is a heavenly adventure!

How are you being conformed or transformed today? Can you see in yourself evidence of true and lasting transformation? And can others see it?

17

My Joy! My Joy!

Mourning may last through the night, but joy comes in the morning.

—Psalm 30:5, paraphrased

From our first conversations about marriage and family, Steve and I agreed that we wanted at least four children, but ideally five. There was no mystical moment associated with that decision—it simply was a mutual desire. After Jessica and Rebekah were born, we experienced the sorrow of losing our third baby, Grace Ann, who was prematurely stillborn. There was no warning to us and no concise medical cause for her death—she died in my womb before she breathed her first breath on this earth.

Then there was the birth of Andrew, and we felt in many ways that our family was complete. We had two beautiful and vivacious daughters and a precious baby boy. And then Andrew died.

Steve and I fully believed that we had and *still* have four children—two living on the earth with us and two in heaven with the Lord, yet we felt incomplete in our desires for our family.

When we learned that I was pregnant for the fifth time, we had hopes, of course, for another little boy. That was not God's plan, and from the moment that our baby girl was laid in our arms, we had absolutely no doubt that this child was *exactly* right for our family.

Bethany Joy Swift was born beautiful and healthy on December 30, 1987, about two years after Andrew died.

We gave our daughter the name Bethany because that was the name of the town where Jesus' best friends, Martha, Mary, and Lazarus lived. We wanted our daughter to be best friends with Jesus. We gave her the middle name of Joy because the Lord promises in His Word that even though sorrow may come in the night, joy comes in the morning! Bethany was our joy that came after our "night" of sorrow and mourning. Joy truly was the hallmark character trait of her life—her daddy called her "My joy, my joy!"

As Bethany grew up, we saw in her an obvious gift of serving. Even as a little girl, she would come into a room and ask our guests if she could bring them a cup of tea—she truly became like Martha, who hosted Jesus in her home in Bethany.

When Bethany was a senior in high school, Steve and I often traveled between Tulsa, Oklahoma, and Arkansas to set up a medical clinic in Bentonville, and we would usually return home late at night. We always found that Bethany had laid out our nightclothes and had cut flowers and put them in a vase in our bedroom. It was amazing! Who was this child? The best part about this was that she laid the pajamas and robes with the sleeves folded in fun positions, as if telling a story.

As much as Bethany embodied some of the traits of Martha, she was mostly like Mary, who delighted in sitting at the feet of Jesus, adoring Him and hanging on His every word. From her earliest years, Bethany had a deep love for the Lord.

When Bethany was born, Andrew's nursery became her nursery. For Andrew, I had painted a pastoral mural on all four walls that depicted the relationship between Jesus, the Good Shepherd, and us, His sheep, complete with scriptures. Bethany inherited Andrew's room just as it was, sleeping in the crib where he had last slept.

For six weeks, Bethany never slept at night while she was in her room. Jessica, only twelve years old at the time, would relieve us sometimes during the nights so that we could sleep for several hours undisturbed. Exhausted and bewildered, we went out for an evening and asked dear friends of ours to watch the girls. When we got home, our friend David said, "That's not

Bethany's room. It is still Andrew's. There is a spirit of mourning in there and she senses it. She doesn't feel peace."

My first thought was, *"She's just a newborn baby."* This is true, but we are created and born with specific gifts and callings in our spirit. Those intuitive God-given gifts are there at birth so that we will grow up in them and think of them as normal. Still, Bethany was just an innocent baby girl.

The question was then what we could do about it. David told us, "Anoint the room with oil—doors, windows, murals, and furniture, particularly the crib, and consecrate the room to the Lord and Bethany. If that doesn't work, we'll paint the walls."

As we proceeded to carry out David's advice, I remembered the scriptures in Exodus in which Moses anointed everything in the tabernacle, consecrating it all to the Lord for His presence and glory to abide there. As we anointed Bethany's room, we invited the presence of the Lord to occupy her room.

That night and every night after, Bethany slept throughout the whole night! In fact, her peaceful sleep was so deep we would have to go to her room most mornings and wake her up, from the time she was a baby until she was a teenager. Some things never change!

Let me mention that Bethany was not any more special or spiritually sensitive than her two older sisters. Jessica, the one who loved to climb trees to leave love notes to Jesus, still writes about her love to Jesus and other articles on deeply intriguing and convicting subjects today. As a mother of three, she is truly a servant-leader in her world of prayer, school, and soccer. Rebekah would drive her piano teachers crazy because she wouldn't read the music but would just wait patiently for her teacher to play the pieces assigned to her. Then, having heard how the pieces should sound, she, in turn, would play them almost flawlessly. Today, Rebekah lives in Nashville and is a singer, songwriter, and mother of three. She has produced two worship albums and two lullaby albums. Our daughters are both beautiful and darling women, lovers of God and His kingdom, and amazing wives and mothers.

But back to our little joy . . . Bethany was so funny and always kept us laughing. For years, as a little girl, she truly believed she had once been an African-American baby. She wanted African-American baby dolls to play with, which was perfectly fine with us; however, nothing we said could budge her from her perspective about what she was like as a baby.

One day as Bethany and I were waiting in the airport for Steve to get home, she saw an African-American family also waiting. She made a beeline for them. As I was trying to catch her, without being too obvious about it, I heard her say, "Hi! I used to be a black baby." They replied, "Really?" She said, "Yes, but then I got Jesus in my heart and now I am white."

What does one say at such an awkward and embarrassing moment? I grabbed her hand and mumbled some words to this rather confused family. I said something like, "She's learning the gospel of Jesus in Sunday school and they use different colors to teach the gospel," and then I just stopped. I said, "I'm sorry Bethany bothered you." The family, now smiling, said, "We understood. No problem—we love her boldness." Oh my . . . boldness was an understatement, but a very prophetic picture of how Bethany would grow up—loving Jesus enthusiastically, worshipping Him with her songs extravagantly, and waiting for her friends to arrive at our home while sitting on the roof outside of her bedroom to chuck tangerines at them when they walked up! She found it quite fun and so did they . . . at least I think they did.

Mature beyond Her Years

Bethany was mature beyond her years for all of her life. She could easily converse with every adult she met. It usually was Bethany who would ask the questions and the adults would answer them, all in a casual and easygoing manner. Steve and I attended a large downtown church, where we were active in a Sunday school class of people our age and a bit older. Bethany was active in youth activities with peers from a former church, and she continued with her youth pastor until the day she left for college. In fact, he was there at our home to tell her good-bye as we drove her to university—what a pastor!

Even though she loved her group, Bethany wanted to attend our adult Sunday school with us. She was quick to enter into discussions and respond to questions from the teacher. She was very comfortable, and the adults lavished her with attention and love.

On one occasion when Steve and I were away and knew we wouldn't make it back to Tulsa in time to pick Bethany up from school, we asked a trusted friend if he would pick her up and bring her to our home. He was delighted to help us, although he admitted to us later, "I had been wondering how I might entertain her or talk to her as I drove her to your home."

"And?" I asked.

He responded, "I didn't have to worry at all about what to say to Bethany. She led the way, asking me questions about my life and childhood and likes and dislikes. She was the interviewer, and I truly enjoyed sharing my experiences with her and seeing and hearing her reactions. Anytime you need a chauffeur for her in the future, count me in!"

Although I homeschooled Bethany during elementary school, when she was in seventh grade, we enrolled her at a well-respected Christian school when we left the bright lights of Dallas and moved to Tulsa.

She had grown up around her older sisters and their friends all her life, and she had a strong affinity for those who were several years older. This social ability, however, did not serve her well on one particular school trip out of the state. I suppose she experienced that typical state of mind of being too big for her britches! When we heard about her misbehavior with a few other girls, Steve and I grounded her for a month and her new private school experience was evaluated against an even more private school called *homeschool!*

Bethany responded as well to the discipline as anybody could expect—she made a 180-degree turn and soon was involved in the worship team and school government. By the time she was a junior in high school, she was writing songs and singing them during the school's chapel services. Both at school and church, she was a vital part of the praise and worship team. She developed a close group of friends and amazed us with her maturity as a teen. Her name, Bethany Joy, truly became her hallmark—she was a worshipper, a true servant, and a friend who loved to laugh and have fun.

Along with a group of other young people primarily led by Sean Feucht, Bethany was part of "Burn Tulsa"—a twenty-four-hour prayer initiative. It was the type of activity and leadership opportunity that suited her fully.

The Beautiful Maid of Honor

Both Jessica and Rebekah got engaged the year that we moved from Dallas to Tulsa, and the following year, in 2001, they had a double wedding. They each had their own bridesmaids and unique wedding dresses, but Bethany served as the maid of honor for both of them!

We could not find a church in our city that would allow an outside pastor to conduct the wedding ceremony. Each girl wanted a different pastor to conduct her wedding vows—one had a pastor from England, and the other had one from Kansas City. We finally talked to Bill Mason, the pastor at Tulsa's Asbury United Methodist Church at the time, who assured us he would serve as the third pastor to pronounce the couples married, in order to satisfy the requirements for an Oklahoma wedding license.

Bethany was beautiful and so poised at the age of thirteen. She adored her big sisters and it was such a gift for her to be able to honor them both so well.

"Go Do Your Dream"

It was the summer before Bethany's senior year in high school when the ownership and administration of Springer Clinic changed. Just months before the announcement of the new ownership, Steve had been given great accolades for the work he had done in turning the clinic around and growing it. When he received word that his job was being eliminated, the news was a complete shock.

Neither of us was eager to start over, yet again, but starting over didn't seem to be problematic to Bethany. By that time in her life, she had already started over several times.

Bethany was nine years younger than her oldest sister and she grew up almost as an only child. Every member of our family doted on her, and once both of her older sisters were away at college, she truly was an only child in our home. She routinely traveled with Steve and me as we went to various business meetings, so she always seemed very informed about Steve's career as a hospital administrator and the administrator of a multispecialty clinic. Even as we took trips to see unique cities, historical sites, and the beautiful countryside, Bethany would be in the backseat of the car attentively listening to Steve and me discuss what we called the "sick-care" business, and how someday we were going to change the direction of health care and lead a "quest for wellness."

"Where are the doctors who want to get to the root causes of sickness and disease, and move their patients into a preventive lifestyle of good nutrition and health? Where are the medical clinics with our kind of vision?" we asked ourselves openly and often.

Bethany heard it all, quietly listening and sleeping, as we speculated about when we might create our dream medical clinic to address our concerns.

> *"Daddy, don't go get just another job, go do your dream!"*
>
>

When Steve was given the news of his release, we were dumbfounded, bewildered, and honestly scared. How and where would we start over? How would we get ready again to move to a new city, make new friends, and reestablish ourselves with Bethany as she was starting her senior year of high school? How, how, how?

It was Bethany, our wise eighteen-year-old, who said boldly, "Daddy, don't go get just another job, go do your dream!" Wow! The Lord's wisdom to us came out of the mouth of a teenage girl.

Sometimes we hear the Lord better when we are not entangled in what-if and if-only. Bethany was so secure in her heavenly Father's love and sufficiency that she could hear Him clearly! She was also secure in our love for each other and for her.

Let me rewind the story a bit and go back to a significant event that had happened about six years earlier—this particular incident took place on the last Sunday that our family was in Dallas. The movers were coming the next day, and we would be in Tulsa within hours. We attended our beloved church as a family for the last time, with Jessica and Rebekah attending as well.

The church had a guest speaker that weekend, a prophetic man who had spoken around the world and had written several books. He didn't know us, and we didn't know him personally, only by reputation.

At the end of his sermon, this prophet looked out over the congregation and singled out our family. We were the only ones he spoke to publicly that morning. He began with, *"I see a rainbow over this entire family, the work of each of you will be marked by great promise and success."* Then he continued, speaking a definitive word of promise to each family member. Times like this are such a wonderful reminder of our amazing God, who is and ever will be revealing Himself and how well He knows us.

And now there we were, six years later, beginning the pursuit of our dream.

We found investors and identified the specifications and designs that we wanted for our clinic. We decided to locate the clinic in Bentonville, Arkansas.

We found a building that was at the shell stage of construction, which enabled us to finish the building according to our unique plans. The property we had found was located on Rainbow Curve. We were in awe—God sometimes has an amazing sense of humor, and the prophecies He gives are *always* accurate. We were under His rainbow of promise!

Words for Reflection

"From the rising of the sun to its going down the Lord's name is to be praised" (Psalm 113:3).

"This is the day that the Lord has made; we will rejoice and be glad in it" (Psalm 118:24).

> *Praising and rejoicing are decisions, not feelings or circumstances. What will you rejoice in and praise God for today?*

"I have set My rainbow in the clouds, and it will be the sign of the covenant between me and the earth" (Genesis 9:13 NIV).

> *Prophecies are God's promises to come, and truths that He wants revealed to us. Some prophecies spoken to you may not come to pass immediately, as it was in our family's case; but every word spoken by the prophet to every member of our family did come to pass. When we found the brand-new building located on Rainbow Curve, we remembered the unconditional promise of God that He would never leave us or forsake us, but He would instead lead us through our journey on earth. And that is exactly what He did. He led us to Rainbow Curve where He established our dream that remains today at this writing.*

18

Growing Up...
with Mom and Dad

"Bethany's House"

When we first moved to Tulsa, we lived in a condominium for about a year while we searched for land to buy and made plans to build a home. When the architect's rendering came back after eight months of design work and alterations, the project had swelled in cost to a lot more than we were prepared to spend.

When I went to see the property on which we had been hoping to build our third dream home, I was disappointed about our failed plans, to say the least. It was such a beautiful piece of property that overlooked a valley. As I drove sadly away from the site, I saw a house just down the road with a "For Sale by Owner" sign—the owners were just putting the sign in the yard as I drove by. I stopped and asked if I could call my husband and daughter and have them come and see the home with me right then. They happily agreed.

I had the brilliant idea that I could act as my own contractor for the new house while living in the "fixer-upper" a few blocks away. I had supervised the designing and building of three homes at that point, I had a degree in interior design from a major university, and I knew how to work directly with plumbers and electricians and all of the other subcontractors needed to build a beautiful home. In the meantime, the house for sale seemed like a good possibility that we could sell for a profit once our home was done.

When Steve and Bethany arrived, the owners gave us time to walk through the house by ourselves—I hated it! But Steve saw potential and Bethany loved it—I felt as if I was living out a scene in *Goldilocks and the Three Bears*.

Thanking the owners, we told them we would let them know our decision later that day. As we drove away to go back to our condo, I shared my ideas about self-contracting while living in that house and selling it at the end—as soon as we built our home on the beautiful lot, we would sell the home for a profit. It was a win-win for us, or so I presumed.

After listening to my grand plan, Bethany said, "Well, I like it and I wouldn't mind living in it forever." She was just twelve years old. I said, "Get over that idea, Bethany. It is awful." She came back with, "Mom, you need a lesson in gratefulness." Steve remained silent—a wise man—and we made an offer on the home later that day. The owners accepted it, the plan was in motion, and we started the process of moving out of the temporary condo that we had been in for over a year.

Silently, I was disheartened, but I also knew that years ago I had made an agreement with the Lord that I would never exchange the eternal blessing of peace and joy for something as temporal as a house. I knew we had only six more years with Bethany living at home before she would go to college, and if she loved the house, I would learn to like it. I also began to see *why* she liked it—the upstairs bedroom she chose for herself had a large bay window topped by a turret on the exterior. Her bedroom was large and beautiful with an outstanding view of evening sunsets, and the turret shape made it feel like a castle that was perfect for her as a princess . . . and for chucking tangerines at her slumber-party guests!

College, Here She Comes!

We ended up living in that house with Bethany until she finished her senior year at Metro Christian Academy. At the end of the summer after she graduated, we all—her two older sisters and brothers-in-law included—packed up Bethany's new car and our cars to move her to Oklahoma Baptist University (OBU) in Shawnee, Oklahoma.

As we were loading the cars with everything that she was bringing with her, she said, "Now Mom, don't sell this house just because I'm going off to college."

I said, "Why would you think that?"

She quickly responded, "Because when I went away to summer camp one year, you got rid of my cat!" In truth, I had never liked that cat, and I thought the cat ought to go to a permanent summer camp as well. I assured her that we would keep the house for her to come home to during her college years.

David Bendett, her high school youth pastor, had come early that morning to hug her, say good-bye, and tell her that he had taken a pastoral position with a church in Corpus Christi, Texas. He wanted to be the one who told her so that she wouldn't hear it through the grapevine. David was much more than just her youth pastor; he was now our family's close friend. He had discipled Bethany well—he exemplified passionate discipleship and extravagant worship, both qualities that Bethany warmly embraced. She waved good-bye to him and cried as we drove away from our home to move her into college.

The whole family came with us to move Bethany in. We unpacked her stuff, and then her sisters set up her college room and met her roommate. Once everything was settled, we went to get Mexican food, and then returned to campus as the upperclassmen were handing out beanies to the freshmen for orientation. Her sisters hugged and kissed her, and her brothers-in-law patted her on the back. As she walked off with her beanie on her head, she looked back at us with tears in her eyes. We all turned away with our own tears so she wouldn't see.

A Night to Remember

Just a couple months after Bethany began classes at OBU, the school hosted a parent's weekend, so we went to visit her. Bethany told us just as we were getting ready to return to Tulsa that she was going to be in the Freshman Follies talent show that night. We were so excited for her, and although she insisted that it wasn't a big deal, we stayed for the show.

We had seen Bethany play the piano and lead worship many times. Most every night when we were getting into bed, we could hear Bethany upstairs playing and singing, but we didn't know that she was writing songs as well. So, it *was* a big deal for us, especially when we learned that she and a new friend were singing one of her songs. When they were done singing, parents and students stood in applause. Here are the lyrics:

> Have you ever been hurt so bad
> You don't care to see the rising sun?
> What other shadows have turned to stone?
> Say good-bye to your joy and happiness.
>
> You've gotta forgive and forget
> Or you'll never see the new day dawning.
> You've gotta forgive and forget
> Or you'll never know where life is calling.
>
> Don't look at what you've lost,
> But look at what you've gained.
> Don't look at what you've lost,
> But look at what remains.
>
> When you've been hurt by someone,
> They hold a power over you,
> Until you close the door to the pain,
> The broken pieces of life remain.
>
> Learn to smile, learn to laugh again,
> Free yourself, only you can win.
> You've gotta forgive and forget,
> Or you'll never see a new day dawning.
> —Bethany Swift, "Forgive and Forget"
> Played and sung by Bethany at the
> OBU Freshman Follies event in 2006

We left Shawnee late that night so full of pride and joy. Who was this girl? She was so remarkable at the young age of eighteen years old. Bethany was going to come home the following weekend to see her sister Rebekah, who was going to be visiting Tulsa.

Steve, for some strange reason, had felt our family needed to get together and had asked Rebekah and her husband, Luke, to come for a visit, although Luke wasn't able to because of his work schedule. Steve, Jessica, Rebekah, Bethany, two-year-old Lydia (Jessica's oldest daughter), and I spent a glorious fall morning at the Philbrook Museum of Art that following weekend, touring the exhibits and the fabulous new Italian gardens, and taking pictures galore. We finished our morning enjoying the lunch buffet. When it was time for Bethany to return to OBU on Sunday afternoon (she didn't want to leave), Rebekah hugged her good-bye and said, "I'll see you in two weeks for Thanksgiving. Study for your finals and finish strong."

Bethany called from school the following Thursday and told us that she wanted to come home again for a visit. We were leaving the next day to go to Van Buren, Arkansas, to visit friends for the weekend. I told her that it made far more sense to me that she should stay in Shawnee and study for her upcoming exams. I reminded her that in less than a week she would be driving to Tulsa for Thanksgiving, and would get to be with her sisters, brothers-in-law, and her little niece. She agreed, but very reluctantly.

Words for Reflection

"The faithful love of the Lord never ends! His mercies never cease. Great is his faithfulness; his mercies being afresh every morning" (Lamentations 3:22–23 NLT).

Reflect: The past is for wisdom, the future is for hope, but today is for joy!

Declare the joys of today that you find, regardless of the day.

19

The Call in the Night

Steve and I did go to Arkansas for the weekend and had a great day on Saturday with our friends. The guys played golf, while we girls shopped—nothing unusual about that scenario. That night, my friend Barbara and I went to see a movie, and the guys and Shelia stayed home to watch a ballgame. As we were leaving the theater around nine thirty, I called Bethany to check on her and encourage her to study hard for finals. Then I said, "See you in a few days."

Later that night, as we were sleeping in our friend's guest bedroom, *the call* came at two o'clock.

Totally unexpected.

Fiercely *unwanted*.

The call shattered our world, yet again.

Our beloved Bethany had been killed in an automobile accident just after midnight in Stillwater, Oklahoma. She died instantly.

Perfect children aren't always perfect, but it still seemed abnormal to us that Bethany had been out in Stillwater, not in Shawnee studying like we thought. Why was she out on the road after midnight? She knew our cardinal family rule to never be in a car after midnight—a rule that had been firmly established when the older girls began to drive and date. Our minds were reeling . . . why, why, why?

Jessica and Rebekah were wonderful big sisters and exceptional role models for Bethany—they are beautiful inside and out. Both were also academically exceptional, even receiving scholarships for college. Jessica seemed to be routinely chosen for leadership positions and Rebekah's musical talents were well acknowledged in the music conservatory at the University of Missouri-Kansas City, where she went to school.

To our credit, Steve and I provided a home that honored God and His Word, the Bible. We began teaching all of our daughters to memorize scripture at the age of three. I can still remember the first verse that I taught Jessica— "This is the day that the Lord has made. I will rejoice and be glad in it."

We were also strict about the friendships the girls made, and our daughters were quick to come talk to us about their thoughts and concerns. All of the girls adored their daddy and respected him. He put it in their hearts to not settle for just any ole guy. They knew they were valued by us and he wanted the very same value to be within their marriages. Early in the girls' lives, Steve began praying for the men who one day would fall madly in love with and want to marry our daughters. Believe me, we set the standard high, and today, we have two of the finest sons-in-law imaginable. Both love God deeply, and love and adore their wives. Both are super dads to each of their three children. Both admire, respect, and love us.

Parents of daughters couldn't ask for more, but remember that we, particularly Steve, had prayed for this from the time they were born until the day he walked them down the aisle to marry their chosen mates.

The bottom line is that you can't stay in the questions that have no answers. A person who suffers this kind of loss must move quickly into God's grace and mercy, whether or not they have understanding or an answer to why.

All of these memories and policies in our home came in like a flood to compound all of our questions of why and how. Most of the questions had no answers and still don't. As we pieced the story together as well as we could, we learned that the girl who lived next door to Bethany had come to her distraught over what she believed was a pending breakup with her boyfriend, who was at Oklahoma State University in Stillwater. She begged Bethany to go with her to Stillwater to find him in the hope that she could talk to him and persuade him not to break up with her. How do such minor things become so major? The girl was only eighteen years old!

However, our little "Martha," with her gift of service, agreed without a second thought to our instructions to stay in Shawnee and use that time to study for finals. They went from party to party to find this young man. A group of kids knew where he was and said they were going there, and that Bethany, as the designated driver, could follow them in the girl's car.

She made a wrong turn and as she was turning around to cross the highway, she didn't see a pickup truck coming over the hill. The driver hit Bethany's side. She broke her neck and died instantly. The passenger was thrown out of the car and badly injured, but she lived.

Bethany's gift of service was real. She was motivated to serve in ways that I would never want to, and she served in ways that we only learned about after her death. Oh, the Bethany stories we heard from her friends, peers, and parents! But when all is said and done, she moved outside of wisdom, and drove to Stillwater instead of staying at OBU to study as we had advised.

Trust makes us dangerous and is a powerful weapon against Satan. Trust makes us lean in when the world says, "Stand in your own strength—buck up!"

Eighty-eight days into her freshman year, Bethany's life on this earth ended. We as her parents have beaten ourselves up with "why" and "what-if" speculations. The bottom line is that you can't stay in the questions that have no answers. A person who suffers this kind of loss must move quickly into God's grace and mercy, whether or not they have understanding or an answer to why.

We received the first call about the accident from a friend of Bethany's who told us she *may* have been in a car accident. We immediately called one of our dearest friends who was the hospital administrator at the hospital where the ambulance had taken Bethany. He quickly got dressed and went to the emergency room, where he called us back and confirmed her death.

When Steve got off the phone and told me, I was reeling. I felt as if I was spiraling down into a dark abyss. I said, "Lord, this one is going to kill me. I'll never make it through."

And then, I heard Him say, *"My ways are higher."* I responded, "I don't know how anything high can come out of this, but I trust you." Immediately, I felt a peace come around me.

Trust makes us dangerous and is a powerful weapon against Satan. Trust makes us lean in when the world says, "Stand in your own strength—buck up!" That night I felt like I had no strength to do anything, but I could will to trust.

Pastor Bill Johnson of Bethel Church says, "Faith stands on the shoulders of quiet trust." Stop for a moment, and really think about that statement.

The Bible says that it is impossible to please God without faith. How can we have faith and believe in something or someone if we can't trust or see? The peace that surpasses understanding comes when we give up our rights and trust God. *Period!* He knows how to maneuver us through the dark. He sees! He knows! He understands!

Trust and Faith Are a One-Two Knockout Punch to Satan

When I heard God's voice say *"My ways are higher,"* it was out of my spirit—not my mind—that I responded, "I trust you, Lord." There was no pause to think, and no attempt to rationalize or spiritualize, because I was spiraling down into the darkest, deepest pit imaginable. I wanted to die, right then and right there. It was a response to a deathblow when I said, "I trust you!" Faith was standing on trust. I surrendered to trusting God, the Creator of life on this earth and in heaven. Faith was denying the influence of death over me and in me.

I gave up, in a moment, my right to ever understand *why,* and I yielded to my faith in God, who I know is good and able to sustain me. I trusted God, and light broke through my darkness and hopelessness. That "peace that surpasses understanding" began to seep into and fill my desperate soul.

Just before sunrise, our other dear friends David and Connie from Van Buren picked us up from the home of the friends we were visiting. David drove Steve's car and Connie followed us in their car back to Tulsa. As the sun began to rise, breaking forth with early-morning light, Steve began proclaiming the same verse he had proclaimed for so many years while driving the girls to school: "From the rising of the sun to its going down, the Lord's name is to be praised" (Psalm 113:3). I joined with him. We both knew we had to *say* what we knew we believed even if we didn't feel it—that no matter how dark the night, the sun always rises with light.

As the sun rose and became more brilliant in the sky, it stood as evidence that as long as this old earth exists, the sun *will* rise and dispel the darkness. Slowly, as were being driven home by our friends, we began to catch our breath and believe that we wouldn't die, but live!

One of Bethany's songs, which we had never heard, but apparently was sung in chapel services at Metro Christian Academy, was "Hallelujah to the Lamb," although the kids at school called it "Bethany's Song." A copy of the song was given to us by Tayler, one of Bethany's dearest high school friends, who was part of the worship team at school with her. Rebekah played and sang it at Bethany's memorial service. How did she give such a sacrificial offering? I still don't know—such grace!

> All my days may You watch over me.
> May Your lamp of glory shine on me.
> Draw me deeper to intimacy.
> Drench my heart with the stream of Your oil.
>
> I will lift up my praise to the heavens,
> To the Creator of all beings.
> Hallelujah to the Lamb,
> Praise be to Him!
>
> May I always rescue the poor.
> May I make the widow's heart sing,
> Be the eyes to the blind,
> Feet to the lame, and father to the needy.
> —Bethany Swift, "Hallelujah to the Lamb"

Bethany first sang this song in public during her senior year of high school in a chapel service.

Rebekah, her husband, and Don Chaffer from the band Waterdeep later recorded a small album called *The Gift of Song*. It is a compilation of songs written by Bethany and various other singer-songwriters. It includes Bethany's songs "Hallelujah to the Lamb" and "Forgive and Forget."

Words for Reflection

"Though He slay me, yet will I trust Him" (Job 13:15).

Great testimonies and acts of faith are slowly distilled predispositions based upon having heard and accepted God's truth and faithfulness. They are not contrived so much in the moment but brought forth by the Spirit of God, for us to then declare them by faith.

We cannot allow—we must not allow—past experiences to influence our trust or faith in a God who is truly good and really there. We must declare our faith now in the Lord's sufficiency to sustain us and uphold us and redeem us no matter what.

20

Bethany's Memorial

Bethany's memorial service was held at First United Methodist Church, where Steve and I had begun attending barely a year before. A friend told us later, "I'm glad you were at First Methodist. There isn't another beautiful sanctuary in Tulsa that could have held all the people who came to that service." The sanctuary's majestic beauty and stained-glass windows that allowed rainbow colors to come through only added to the glory of God's eternal love and grace.

Students, faculty, and parents came from OBU and Metro Christian Academy. Bethany's lifelong friends came, including her friends from her youth group and even the girl who was in the car wreck with her—she insisted that her parents bring her from Dallas for the service, even though she was battered and on crutches.

Steve and I are aware that many couples who lose a child to death struggle to keep their marriage together, but we do not consider ourselves to be experts on how a marriage cannot only survive but continue to thrive after the deaths of *three* children.

How does a person, couple, or family survive the death of a child? "Survive" is a very relative word. It was never our desire or hope to survive. We wanted our girls and ourselves to thrive! Our goal was that we would come through this devastation in triumph. Why? Because we believe that through our faith, through our trust in the Lord, and through our counting on grace and mercy in an empowering and real God, we would not be devastated in sorrow and loss. As our good friend always said, "It's all Jesus." I believe this, or I certainly would not have voluntarily endured the anguish of writing this book.

This book is about a real relationship with a real God. I have written it to be **raw, real, and relevant.** There is no fluff or exaggeration—it is what it is. That is like life; since we don't get to create the day, we just get to live it.

Both Steve and I had strong individual faith prior to the death of any of our children, and we still have this faith today!

Our faith together as a married couple enabled us to build our family on faith, which we are still maintaining today.

We were involved in churches through our years of marriage where we had friends who reinforced our faith, endured hardship with us, and shored us up.

We turned to each other and to the Lord in our grief, leaving blame of any sort, however little, out of our thoughts and conversations.

Lastly, when human strength and initiative have failed, the Lord has not!

A Focus on Earthly Reality

As time passed after Bethany died, the day came when I decided to do the very thing that I told Bethany I would not do—sell the house! It did not matter now, since Bethany wouldn't be coming home. Who cared? Well, as it turns out, Steve did, and that was a bit of a stumbling block for me. But I was convinced that it was time to leave behind the vivid memories of "Bethany's House," and besides, I never liked the house anyway. I had completely convinced myself that I was going to sell our house and leave behind my anger and grief over Bethany's death. I figured that Steve would come around to the idea, probably because he is a peacemaker, and he loved me more than the house!

It was about nine months after Bethany's death when Steve had gone out of town on a weekend golfing trip with some friends that I was left, for the first time, by myself. I threw a pity party, and of course, this "party" got bigger as the night went on.

Bethany and her dad loved this house, but I did not. I made plans about how I would announce to Steve when he got back that we were going to sell it. I rehearsed what I would say and how I would say it so that I would get the answer I was seeking. As I completed scheming, the doorbell rang. Unannounced, my next-door neighbor, Ben Ferrell, a godly man in the television and music industries, came over. I invited him in and as we sat and chatted about menial stuff, he suddenly said, "Judy, I hope you won't be too eager to sell this house." How could he even know that it was me, not Steve, who was considering such a move?

> *"Truth, Lord, I would rather have your glory no matter what. I wouldn't trade your presence for bricks and mortar!"*

He went on to say, "Through the years, I have heard the praise music coming from various groups singing in your backyard. I have seen you baptize young adults in your pool. I have heard and watched celebration parties of all sorts and sizes take place in your backyard. *This is a special place God has used, and still wants to use, for His glory. Don't be too quick to move."* He then got up from the chair and left, just like that!

Stunned, I closed the front door, went back to my chair, sat down, put my face in my hands, and cried and cried. I called out to God, *"Truth, Lord, I would rather have your glory no matter what. I wouldn't trade your presence for bricks and mortar!"*

Then the Lord reminded me of how much Bethany had loved the house and the songs she had written from the piano room. The Lord reminded me that Steve and our other two daughters loved the house. It was and is a great home for our grandkids, guests, family, and friends to gather, no matter how many of us there are, what the event is, or the time of day. We would stay in "Bethany's House," and transform it into our home. I knew that even though Steve would have moved if that was what I wanted or needed, leaving or running away would not have solved my pain or sorrow. Staying and waiting on God and having time to heal my broken heart until I could embrace this house was the higher call for our lives.

In the weeks that followed, I began making the plans for the renovations to the kitchen and the master bathroom, with a few other changes to the interior of the house that would make it feel and look more like what I wanted. I discovered that when you see a place as God's chosen place, it will become your place as well. And so it has!

Bethany saw angels and demons when she was a little girl, teenager, and young adult. She talked about them, which we neither encouraged or discouraged; to her, the kingdoms of spiritual beings were a normal part of life. We knew she had an awareness of the spiritual realm that was not average.

A young prophet friend, Shawn Bolz, came to visit us several times when Bethany was younger. We would always give him Bethany's room. On one occasion, he told us the next morning that he could hardly sleep the night before. He said that there was so much supernatural activity in that room that it kept him awake all night.

> *I had to will to walk in His grace—it is still my choice, my will, and what I will choose.*

The first time this happened, he asked Bethany, who was only ten years old, "Do you see angels?" She said, "Yes, some of them are very big."

He replied, "Those are probably principalities, not ordinary angels." *What a casual, yet uncommon conversation the two of them had!* The difference didn't really matter to Bethany, nor was it particularly intriguing to her. At that point, she was comfortable enough with her relationship with supernatural beings, and as long as they were "good angels," she accepted them as a normal part of her reality.

I thought about Bethany's relationship with the supernatural world a great deal after she died. Having a child like Bethany made it easier, I think, to imagine Bethany with the Lord in eternity. I had full assurance that she felt right at home among the heavenly beings there, and with her big sister and brother! Let me say, once again I had *to will* myself to look beyond, and focus on Jesus and His heavenly kingdom. I had to will to walk in His grace—it is still my choice, my will, and what I will choose.

Words for Reflection

"In the year of King Uzziah's death I saw the Lord sitting on a throne, lofty and exalted, with the train of His robe filling the temple. Seraphim stood above Him, each having six wings: with two he covered his face, and with two he covered his feet, and with two he flew. And one called out to another and said, 'Holy, Holy, Holy is the Lord of hosts, the whole earth is full of His glory'" (Isaiah 6:1–3 NASB).

"Worthy are You, O Lord; worthy are You, O God, to receive glory and honor and power" (Revelation 4:11 Voice).

"For He shall give His angels charge over you, to keep you in all your ways" (Psalm 91:11).

It was as I was thinking about this scripture one day and worshipping, that I saw God's robe flowing down until it enveloped me. I thought to myself, "Wow! Lord, even your robe touches us on earth," and I remembered the story of the woman in the Bible who was healed when she touched Jesus' robe. When we are desperate and need to be touched, even if it is just His robe, He touches us. That is amazing, healing grace.

Have you ever asked the Lord for a vision, or to see His glory?

Seeing with Spiritual Eyes

Just as the Lord calls us to hear with spiritual ears, He also calls us to see with spiritual eyes!

When the Holy Spirit comes into us, He literally inverts the way we live our lives. People who have not yet received Jesus as their Savior live primarily according to physical instincts and drives, and secondarily by natural reasoning of the mind. However, after we receive Christ and the Holy Spirit, we become spirit, soul (which includes our mind, will, and emotions), and body, in that order, with our spirit ruling our lives. Our spiritual sensitivity is drastically heightened. We begin to hear and see into a realm that was once too dark for us. What an amazing salvation!

God wants us to recognize His presence and to see His activity for what it is, but to do so, we must learn how to see God in the midst of joy as well as tragedy.

I can see a space shuttle lift off and not understand why or how, but nevertheless, seeing it happen lets me know that a space shuttle can escape the bonds of earth's gravity and soar into space, even though it is beyond the capability of my physical eyes to see its final orbit.

Even if we catch only a glimpse of God within the swirl of our confusion and turmoil,

> *Even if we catch only a glimpse of God within the swirl of our confusion and turmoil, it often is enough for us to know that God is present.*

it often is enough for us to know that God is present. When we experience His presence, a bit of the fog in us—brought on by doubts, conflicting advice and opinions, and in many cases, exhaustion both physically and emotionally—lifts. It is when that clarity comes that we are able to proclaim, "God is all in all." He knows all. He governs all. He is present in all moments. And then we can say, "I trust you. Not my will, but yours."

Trust comes when we, in faith, trust the One we normally cannot see, the Lord Jesus. We choose to fix our spiritual eyes on Jesus, who is the author and perfecter of our faith, and not on the circumstances. Remember, it was years before this that I first heard those words of power and promise as I walked down the hospital corridor to see my son for the last time, *"Look beyond what you see and fix your eyes on Jesus, the author and perfecter of your faith."* Christianity requires a faith walk, and Christianity demands trust in the One who is trustworthy.

More times than I like to admit, I have doubted who I was hearing, thinking, "Ah, that's just me, my mind, my emotions." God speaks to us very strategically. His saying *"look beyond"* was a clear word to me that I wasn't looking beyond my horrific pain and circumstances. God's directive was compassionately plain: *"Fix your eyes on me. Don't get distracted."*

A friend of mine once gave me a good analogy about what it means to see with spiritual eyes, after I shared with her what I had heard the Lord say that day in the hospital. She compared it to when she had been in an optometrist's office and was staring at one of those squiggly pictures that show absolutely nothing on the surface. She looked at it long and hard but saw nothing that made sense—only squiggles and confusion. Then, the optometrist's assistant whispered in her ear, "Focus your eyes *beyond* the picture." When she did that, the image slowly came into focus.

When I did that in my life, it was as if the reality of the invisible heavens shifted and opened to me. Nothing had changed in the reality of Andrew's situation, but the focus in *me* changed. I could finally see the Lord in the midst of the mess.

I remember years before when I was praying in a happier moment, the Lord simply said to me, *"I am the Lord your God. I stand before you complete. Complete for all your needs and all your desires. I am your need. I am your desire."* I loved hearing His voice for no particular reason, just reminding me for another time, or perhaps, for this time.

Take a moment to think about your needs and your desires. When are your true needs and desires met outside of the Lord? Do those quick fixes last? When the Lord steps in to meet all your needs and all your desires, He is reminding you, "I am. I am the only One who can really help you."

When a person wants to cross a large lake and then land at a specific destination, he must fix his eyes on that point, because if he does not focus on it, the boat will veer off course.

The same principle is true for our spiritual destiny—our focal point must be Jesus, keeping our eyes on Him. Our dear English friend always says, "Just keep your eyes on the prize!"

Jesus is the author who wrote our life stories, even before we were born. He knows every detail of our lives from conception to the doorway of eternity and beyond. He is the *finisher* of our stories—the One who brings life to a fulfilled and eternal reward. He knows the beginning from the ending and every step and every hour along the way. He does not abandon us in the middle of our story unfolding. He is adequate for all of our needs and desires!

Although I cannot fully imagine everything that must have gone through Peter's mind when he stepped over the side of the boat to walk on the waves toward Jesus, I do know this: he did it! And as long as Peter kept his gaze on Jesus, he walked on the water. It was only when he began to look around at his circumstances—feeling the blustery wind and seeing the billowing waves—that he became distracted, taking his eyes off of Jesus and beginning to sink until Jesus reached out and saved him.

The crises and tragedies of life are the "life storms" that often overwhelm us. It is only by keeping ourselves focused on Jesus' sustaining power and presence that we have the ability to do what seems humanly impossible! We must see Him as the silver lining! He is our bright light and hope in the midst of trouble and along our entire journey.

The Line in the Cemetery Grass

Six years after we buried Andrew's body, I visited Andrew's grave. It was only the second time I had been to his grave. As I stood staring at his grave marker, which was next to the marker laid in place for his sister Grace Ann, the stark reality and finality of the two deaths hit me like a cold wave. I was overwhelmed. Suddenly, it seemed that an invisible finger of God drew a line in the grass of that cemetery. On one side of the line were their gravestones—marking death and finality—and on the other side of the line were unending life and eternal blessing.

The more clearly that I *saw* this invisible line, the more fully I understood God's heart. He hates death because He is life, and that day, the heavenly Father drew the line for me. These deaths were not going to consume me, define me, or darken His light. He had drawn the line, and the schemes of the Enemy were halted. That vision—that *seeing*—once again gave me hope and trust that God still has a future for me.

Does life always turn out exactly the way we planned or wanted? Certainly not. Oh, the speeches I have written in my mind, knowing exactly what I would say and do in every situation. I suspect every playwright imagines how their creation will be on the stage, only to be surprised when things naturally go a bit differently. The key to overcoming life's hardships is not found in our imagination or means of self-comfort, but rather in giving all of a situation and the total control for all of its consequences to the Lord.

We must learn to say, "I choose to trust you, Lord." Say it out loud! Say it to your mind and say it to your emotions: "I choose!" Say it over and over until your soul and body fully align with your will. Look beyond what you see! Seek Him in the midst of the mess, the pain, the sorrow, and the suffering. Trust that there really is a beautiful, clear picture within the mess!

> *"The past is for wisdom.*
> *The future is for hope.*
> *Today is for joy."*

Seeing Life through God's Eyes

We must never lose sight of the truth that God *is* the creator of our lives and His world. Take time to see all of the minute details of flowers, amusing aspects of animal life, and the brilliance of the human body's design. All of creation was designed for Him, by Him, and for us to enjoy with Him. All of the beauty in this world points to Him.

As an artist and designer, I thoroughly enjoy all aspects of the creative process *and* the finished work. I like to finish things, and I like to know how it will look in the end; however, I cannot design tomorrow. I have only been given the plans for today.

A friend once told Steve and me years ago, "The past is for wisdom. The future is for hope. Today is for joy." Those words instantly changed my perspective and anxious heart about life's unfair or unexpected hits. Actually, those words are still the very truth I remember and allow to change my perspective today.

Yesterday is gone! Glean wisdom from the past. Ask yourself, "What did I experience? What did I learn? What would I do differently next time?" If you feel like you did something you regret, reconcile through forgiveness. Repent—which involves changing your mind—and then move on. Tomorrow is coming.

I choose to assess today, including all of the good things and the bad things, and to make adjustments accordingly, by faith. As I fall asleep, I remember that *today* will be the *past* by tomorrow morning.

I remind myself often that today is for joy. The Bible tells me, "The joy of the Lord is my strength!" Joy is what makes me strong to keep on keeping on. I love to have fun and I love to laugh—this is how I've always been—but fun and joy are very different. Joy can yield fun, but just having fun cannot yield joy.

Joy is an eternal aspect of the Lord's nature. He finds joy in us as His people, in spite of our bad choices at times. In His presence is the fullness of joy. There are so many truths about the lasting qualities of joy in God's Word. Do a "joy" word study—it's amazing what you will find.

In contrast to joy, happiness and fun are temporary. When the party is over, so is the laughter. When the feel-good movie ends, so do the smiles. I can choose to remember fun and memorable events, but in the end, nothing is changed in me by remembering. People who seek fun move on to the next fun thing, but the feelings of fun are fleeting, at best. Fun fades with the night, but the joy that comes in the morning from the Lord has a mysterious lasting power. Joyful experiences in God's presence are memories that continue to invigorate and refresh the soul. I remember so clearly my truly joyful experiences—seeing a miracle at God's hand, being at the births of our six grandkids, and the literal feeling of His presence. What joy! These moments are worth replaying in the heart again and again, because each time, there is a renewal of joy.

And yes, there is also hope in the future. What an encouraging word. When I look at our world today, I could easily lose hope, but then I look up, take a deep breath, and pray—I focus "beyond."

Look at the horrific hurricanes, tornadoes, fires, earthquakes, and the ravaging destruction and loss they bring. *Now, focus beyond.* See rescuers saving lives and communities coming together to provide shelter and food. See complete strangers helping and sharing with one another. Beyond the wreckage and mess, if you focus, you can see the mercy and goodness of God being demonstrated through human life. The Lord is always drawing near to every tragedy and disappointment with His love. In that, there is true hope!

There is hope embedded in every promise in the Bible. Against all odds, God allows hope to well up into full-fledged faith. I love looking to Romans 12:12, which says, "*Do not forget* to rejoice, for hope is always just around the corner" (Voice). Hard times may come, but we must choose to rejoice, because hope will not fail to show up!

Seeing God's Glory in Creation

I have a very clear picture in my heart of an intimate and faithful God whose presence can be felt, whose Word can be heard and known, and who delights in revealing Himself through countless examples of beauty that He puts in our paths to enjoy.

I once spent a week in the mountains in Arkansas to work on this book—it was a lovely setting. It was spring and I was taking note of the first wild-flowers and the greenery. One day as I was walking in the woods, I came to a small clearing, and there before me stood a twenty-foot pine tree. All through its branches, a purple wisteria plant in full bloom had woven itself until it reached the very top of the tree.

As I stood there in awe, a gentle breeze caused the beautiful blooms to shimmer, and suddenly everything seemed to stand still as the purple blossoms appeared iridescent with movement. It looked like a purple shimmering waterfall, flowing down the deep-green pine. I could hardly breathe, and I just stood there in wonder. Ah, I was in the presence of the Creator!

That wisteria plant was alive as it shimmered, a reflection of God's nature and His glory. The Holy Spirit let me see the Creator in that plant—it was not just a beautiful, flowering bush. When I remember this moment and get very still, it is as if I am right back there in His presence.

God's love is poured out in splendid, extravagant ways all around us for our "seeing." His creativity is there for our "seeing" and our pleasure. His beauty is designed for us to "see" and enjoy.

I have absolutely no doubt that the Lord wants us to see Him at work in our life and our world. Look for Him! Look beyond what you see and truly focus.

Words for Reflection

"My ways are higher than your ways" (Isaiah 55:9 NLT).

God has so many more ways of getting things done than we can ever know . . . but we can believe in them because we can believe in God's superlative, omnipotent, and all-loving nature!

"Now faith is the assurance of things hoped for, the conviction of things not seen" (Hebrews 11:1 NASB).

It is first and foremost by our faith that we see who God is and what God is capable of doing.

"Now to Him who is able to do exceedingly abundantly above all that we ask or think, according to the power that works in us, to Him be glory in the church by Christ Jesus to all generations, forever and ever. Amen" (Ephesians 3:20–21).

Are you anticipating "abundantly above all [you] ask or think"? God is able!

22

Choices with Sight and Sound

Many things that happen in life are not of our choosing, but the truth remains that we each have an opportunity to choose, when it comes to the decisions that truly matter in this life and in eternity. We have within us the ability to see and hear from a divine perspective, and to make choices along the way. We are not helpless victims. Christ said, "I have come that they may have life, and that they may have it more abundantly" (John 10:10). I think that this abundance lies within eternal perspective, and that every person has the ability to choose life through Jesus Christ.

The ultimate truth about this ability is that we can choose *life* even before we are presented with circumstances that seem doomed to death.

Both Moses and Joshua proclaimed that message to the children of Israel about their future life in the Promised Land. *They put the choice before them, declaring that it was up to them to choose life.* The promise was never that in choosing life they would have all of their problems resolved in the precise way they desired, but rather, in choosing life, God would be fully involved and His life for their eternal spirits was going to be activated. Before they entered eternity, they would enjoy a blessed and abundant life on earth, bringing glory and honor to God.

The Ongoing Battle in the Spiritual Realm

I firmly believe that in every time of trial or tragedy, there exists two opposing forces battling in the spiritual realm.

God speaks very directly in the Bible about the wiles and schemes of the Evil One, who is a consummate liar and the engineer of ongoing assaults against the Lord and the people of this earth. He has the ability to create a great deal of fear, doubt, pain, and confusion. If we give into the Devil's temptation to believe that there is no hope or that God is insufficient, we will find ourselves paralyzed in many ways.

The choices we face when confronting tragedy, hardship, or life-changing decisions always boil down to the clash between truth with confidence and lies with fear, with fear most often at the root of the lie.

The Enemy's goal, it seems, is to put us on a slippery slope. He uses lie after lie, attacks with fear, and then brings in confusion and doubt.

Satan does not have real weapons, he only has lies. He lies to us directly and he lies to us about the insufficiency of God, trying to throw our plumb line of peace off balance!

We need to know that when we have these moments of intense doubt and fear, they are not from God—they are from the enemy of our soul. There are plenty of movies out there that are very successful in graphically portraying good and evil, but man did not come up with this idea. There are truly a good and living God and His angels, and there are truly an evil and living Satan and his demons. We are in spiritual warfare, whether or not we like it or believe it.

The choices we face when confronting tragedy, hardship, or life-changing decisions always boil down to the clash between truth with confidence and lies with fear, with fear most often at the root of the lie.

So, what are we to do when we find ourselves confronted with life's circumstances? The wisdom of the apostle Paul sums the answer up nicely when he says, "Stand . . . and pray" (see Ephesians 6:14,18). We must have firm resolve that we will not give in to the Enemy or be paralyzed by his tactics, and we must pray with a faith that envelops boldness, fervor, and persistence. Pray and keep on praying until an answer or peace comes to you and floods within you.

> *What does God's Word say to us, including when the still, small voice of the Holy Spirit is speaking God's word into our innermost heart?*
>
> *Versus*
>
> *What does the Enemy say, sometimes as a whisper in our mind and sometimes through the words of a careless or evil person?*

It is up to us to discern the speaker, discern the message, and then to make a choice: Is this the truth or a lie? Indecision is no-man's-land, and that is the most dangerous place to be.

How can we discern? I believe that one of the first major clues we have is recognizing whether we are experiencing an atmosphere of darkness related to confusion or a light related to peace.

Darkness is palpable. It shrouds our understanding. It comes with swirling and sometimes violent bouts of fear and confusion. In darkness we often cannot see anything, and we certainly cannot see anything positive, only those things that are negative, oppressive, and hopeless. On the other hand, light shatters darkness, and it is up to us to choose light. And we really do have the power to choose—our will cannot be stolen from us. When we choose light, we will begin to see shafts of truth and gain insights into God's goodness shining in the darkness. The Bible is very clear that Jesus, the Light, always overcomes darkness, but we are the ones who must invite Him into our situation.

Discerning the Work of the Enemy

God and Satan are not equals. Satan is a fallen angel, a creature made by God who rebelled and was cast from God's presence. There are twice as many loyal angels who are directed by God as there are Devil's demons. It isn't an equal fight at all, but we sometimes are misled into thinking that Satan is far more powerful than God is.

Satan is not omnipresent—he can only be in one place at a time.

Satan is not all-powerful—he cannot operate beyond the bounds defined by God.

Satan is not all-knowing—he knows only what he observes and overhears. Our work is to discern, while the Devil's work is to "steal, kill, and destroy." His goals are these:

- ◆ to steal our joy
- ◆ to kill our desire to follow Christ fully
- ◆ to destroy us with guilt, shame, conflict, and sorrow

And if the Devil had been able to shatter me, Steve, and our children, then he would have done a work that extended to our grandchildren, and to every person with whom we have had contact in our church, community, business, and ministry endeavors!

> *Exercising our ability to choose is our responsibility, just as voting is our responsibility to maintain our freedom.*

A Choice Is Always Required

Be assured that a choice is always required. Exercising our ability to choose is our responsibility, just as voting is our responsibility to maintain our freedom. Our loving God gave us the gift of free will. The choice for light and life is proactive, always forward moving, and intentional.

When we confronted the Enemy at the time of Andrew's death, we made a decision as a family that we would live as a family. Steve and I made a renewed commitment that our marriage would live. We decided that we would continue to *live* as Christ's people on this earth as long as we are living on earth. We made a decision that we would walk in a life of hope, healing, and a future.

We did the same thing after Grace's death. We did the same thing after Bethany's death. We chose light by praising God at the rising of the sun on our way back to Tulsa after receiving the news of Bethany's death. We chose to trust the Lord to carry us from darkness into His glorious light. We chose . . .

A spiritual life is a life marked by hope, by faith, by love, by joy, and by a lasting inner peace that can only come from God. All of those markers of a thriving, vibrant spiritual life could have been stripped from us had we not made the decision that we would pursue the light and life offered to us by God in our moment of darkness and despair. I am grateful that the Lord enabled us to make the right choices each time. Remember what our good friend Milt always said, "It's all Jesus!"

Words for Reflection

"Now fear the Lord and serve him with all faithfulness . . . choose for yourselves this day whom you will serve . . . but as for me and my household, we will serve the Lord" (Joshua 24:14–15 NIV).

Each of us has the capacity to hear God's voice. The voice of the Lord always brings a lasting peace and it comes often in a whisper, saying, "This is the way, walk in it."

23

Be Mindful of Words Spoken

In an earlier chapter, I shared about the experience I had with Jessica after she fell from a tree. She suffered a compound fracture that required surgery and she was hospitalized for seven days. After her surgery, the surgeon matter-of-factly told us that the surgery went well, except that they found dirt in her bones. He went on to say that if an infection occurred, there could be an amputation. He added, "Don't worry, that probably won't happen," but then went on to say that because the break occurred near her growth plate, her arm might cease growing. "Only time will tell," he concluded.

I stayed in the hospital, and Steve went home to be with Rebekah. Late that evening as Jessica slept, a strange peace began to settle around me and my faith began to rise. I simply declared aloud to the Lord and to anyone else who might be listening, "My daughter's arm will be completely and perfectly healed. She *will* be healed!"

I sat by Jessica's bed all night, speaking against my fear while speaking my faith in an all-powerful God who has no limitations. I read scriptures aloud to myself and to a sleeping Jessica. Fear will always try to creep in, remind you of the worst thing that could happen, and punch a hole in your gut so that any faith you might have had will run out.

If you can't even remember a promise from the Bible or an encouraging word from a sermon, then just say the name of Jesus over and over. His name is above all names and all situations.

I filled up that hole in my gut with the Lord's promise that "God had not given me a spirit of fear, but of power and of love and of a sound mind." A sound mind—I did not care if any doctor, nurse, or hospital staff heard me quoting and reading scripture out (very) loud! I was not crazy. I was determined to have the mind of Christ, full of faith and full of peace, and I was determined to pray for a miracle.

Speak Words of Testimony

The Bible tells us in Revelation that the believers at the throne of God were overcomers. And how did they overcome? They did it in two ways—through the blood of Jesus and the word of their testimony.

If Jesus Christ is your Savior, you have a *salvation* testimony. If you have received answers to prayer, you have a testimony. If you have experienced a supernatural healing or prayed for someone who was miraculously healed, you have a *healing* testimony. If the Lord has spoken to you or visited you, you have a testimony.

> *My spiritual dreams and encounters with the Lord's presence are my testimonies that confirm that He is supernatural, mystical, and answers prayers, even those of a child.*

I had my first spiritual dream when I was nine or ten years old. I had asked God to show me if He was real, and He showed me in a dream that very night. I have a testimony that He answers a child's prayer.

My first experience with *feeling* the power of His presence was when I was fourteen years old and asked the Lord to help my best friend. I have a testimony that He comes in all ways to help us when we ask Him.

My spiritual dreams and encounters with the Lord's presence are my testimonies that confirm that He is supernatural, mystical, and answers prayers, even those of a child.

The word of my testimony is not a matter of speculation or hope. It is what I know to be the hard-core truth of God, proven through real results and changes, particularly ones that I've experienced within myself.

Because I know what God did for me, through me, and to me, who can say otherwise? When I know what I have dreamed or what I have experienced that has felt mystical but produced the fruit of reality and substance in my life, who can take that away from me?

Testimonies never lose their power. As we speak about them or remember them through time, we are the first to be blessed by a renewal and strengthening of our faith. Our family does not carry a mourning spirit or a spirit of bitterness and resentment. We, individually and as a family, nailed the *what-ifs* to the cross. Those taunting reminders are dead and we as a family are alive!

Our daughters Jessica and Rebekah have not only our family's testimonies but also now, with their husbands and children, they have remarkable testimonies of God's mercies and miracles within their families.

When I counsel or teach, I first use God's Word as a foundation of truth, backed by the testimonies in my life of all the times that God has showed up to rescue me, to inspire my awe of Him, to talk to me, to walk with me, to point out the particulars of His magnificent creation, to give me dreams and visions, to forgive me, and mostly to reveal His love for me in extraordinary ways. I have testimonies of laughing for hours without realizing that He was healing my heart as I laughed. I have testimonies related to the power of prayer, of seeing or hearing about real miracles after I have prayed for individuals. These experiences are all a part of my arsenal that defends and protects my faith.

As we build this arsenal, we must remember that God has already supplied all that we need or will need in Christ and His Word.

Words for Reflection

"For it is the Spirit of prophecy who bears testimony to Jesus" (Revelation 19:10 NIV).

"For the Spirit God gave us does not make us timid, but gives us power, love and self-discipline" (2 Timothy 1:7 NIV).

No one can take away or even challenge your testimony, which is your witness to God's workings in you, to you, for you, and through you. They may think you are crazy, but it's no crazier than seeing real miracles of healing that occur right before your eyes, while you are thinking, "Impossible!" He is a personal God who has a plan and destiny for you—He created you with purpose and for a purpose.

24

Learning to Trust More

One day after I had shared some of my experiences related to Andrew's death at a women's meeting, a person said to me, "I have been thinking about what you said to those men in the conference room of the hospital—how you would always love God but not be willing to serve Him if He did not raise up Andrew. What did you mean, exactly?"

Honestly, I don't remember how I answered her sincere question, but I remember that I was surprised at that moment that out of all the questions she could have asked, she asked that. So, what did I mean?

Thinking back to that very erratic moment in the hospital, I would hope I answered the woman with these thoughts:

That day in that little safe room, I was voicing the conflict going on inside me. I love God with all my heart and always will, yet there have been times that my emotions do not follow as quickly as my commitment to trust His love. Love is a choice, not a feeling.

To serve God is also a choice. I have chosen to serve God because I love Him, and I want to serve in His kingdom.

Yet, when life happens, I find myself often responding in anger. I was bartering with the Almighty and challenging Him. Anger is a poor defense, I know, but it is part of my old nature that is still being transformed—vinegar into sweet wine! But anger is a very slippery slope and on that particular day in the hospital, I was headed in a downward spiral leading to

> *I was desperate and angry, probably at the world and probably at God. However, I knew then as I know now that no matter how deeply low I get, God is deeper still.*

complete darkness and despair. My very bold friend simply stopped the sliding with his words of truth. I had to change my thinking and speaking so that I could reverse the direction I was headed in.

Like love, trust is an act of the will. If in the depths of your soul, you truly believe God is good and that nothing can separate you from His love, then you can trust Him.

I was desperate and angry, probably at the world and probably at God. However, I knew then as I know now that no matter how deeply low I get, God is deeper still. He is not taken by surprise by my still-unredeemed flesh and by my threats. He will never forsake me or turn His back on me because He is love, and His love is perfect and never conditional. He is safe, but He is still the Lord, and because He is the Lord and the King of Kings, it was my place to humble myself, repent, and re-confess that I would always love Him and serve Him.

When we exercise our will to come to that place in our submission and honor to God, we are trusting. It is not a position of resignation, but rather, of knowing that God is at work on our behalf. In my times of crisis, I have highly valued those who were *there* for me and those who were not afraid to speak or pray truth in love.

I probably did not answer the woman's earnest question as clearly as I hope that I have written, but it would have been my heart to do so.

Trusting God Is in All Occasions and Situations

Fortunately, we do not get to pick and choose when or where is a good time to practice trust!

At that point in our lives, everything seemed to be going well. God was good! Life was good. Our marriage and family life were good. Steve's job was good—he was the administrator of a large clinic; a health-care business with 125 physicians and 800 employees.

As we were putting down deep roots in Fort Smith, we began building our dream home on some acreage outside of town. And as I explained earlier, that's when the news came that a large firm was buying out the clinic. I had a conversation with the administrative leader of the large firm, and he assured me that I would likely live in our dream home until we retired someday. With that assurance, we went ahead and completed our home on two-and-a-half acres, complete with a pond and a barn for the girls' two horses.

Shortly after that conversation, we took a weekend trip with friends to the Dallas-Fort Worth metroplex for a large Christian conference where the man preaching, whom we did not know personally, called on us out of two thousand attendees by saying that we had two children in heaven. That gave us the confidence that this prophetic speaker was about to tell us something that we did not already know. "You are going to be relocated geographically," he said. We were shocked! I looked at Steve in wonderment, thinking, "What does that man know that you don't know? You are the administrator!" Steve looked just as confused as I felt.

A few days later, Steve and I were headed to Boston for a business meeting. I called a realtor we were friends with, just to see what was going on in the real estate market. She told me that houses the size of ours were not doing well, and if we decided to sell "it would probably be a long wait." My first thought was, "That prophet man really did not know what he was saying."

On our return from this three-day meeting in Boston, we received an envelope from a law firm in our mailbox. Inside the envelope, we found a personal note asking if we would be interested in selling our house. Then, if the letter wasn't shocking enough, we got a call later that evening from our neighbor asking if we would consider selling our home to a couple who had asked them to ask us.

Two contracts bidding for our dream home on two acres with a pond and a barn in a real estate market that was struggling—how amazing is that? But we still disregarded the prophet's word because Steve's company had told us that we wouldn't have to move since they weren't going to relocate us.

If the two bids weren't enough to test our faith or bewilderment, it was only a matter of days until Steve was told by his company that they intended to move him to Dallas so that he could be more centrally located to administer the various clinics that they wanted him to oversee on a regional basis.

Our dream home sold without a realtor to the highest bidder. We sold both horses, horse trailer, and tack, except Jessica's English equestrian saddle, which she wanted to keep; and might I add, we sold them within a week! We moved to Dallas—cats, dogs, and all. We bought a home that was under construction in Dallas and began the work to finish it out.

We had *not* believed the prophet who had spoken to us, telling us we would be relocated, and instead *had* believed the corporate executive who told us we wouldn't be moved and that we should finish our dream home. We had been mistaken on both sides!

However, Father God loves us so much that He will cause *all* things to work together for our good and His glory in spite of ourselves. It was all in God's timing.

We moved to Dallas late that summer—the older girls went back to college, and Bethany, her cats, and the dog went with us.

We were in Dallas for less than a year when Steve's company closed its doors. We were stunned. There had been no clues and no prophet's word—we were unexpectedly jobless! Instead of immediately looking for a job while we still received a severance payment, our pastor suggested that Steve go on a sabbatical to seek God and get perspective. Luckily, the severance payment allowed him to do that. Our pastor arranged for Steve to go to his friend's ranch, and he encouraged Steve not to put a time limit on this time of rest. Steve embraced this counsel wholeheartedly. It seemed like crazy advice, but I agreed to it, too, and that was a miracle in itself.

While he was at the ranch, he rested, took long walks, watched the sunrises and sunsets, and slept long hours. He read and asked God, "Lord, what do you want me to do next? Do you want me in full-time ministry?" The Lord responded to him very clearly, "Yes, I want you in full-time ministry. Go back into the work field I prepared you for and be my full-time minister." It was after clearly hearing from the Lord that Steve then asked the Lord for five job offers in his field of work, but only when it was God's timing.

I stayed in Dallas while Steve was at the ranch resting and hearing from the Lord. I homeschooled Bethany in the various Starbucks coffee shops around Dallas, as we tried to keep ourselves happy and occupied without worrying. When Steve returned to Dallas—refreshed and full of faith—he took golf lessons, read Western novels, had leisurely morning coffee with me, and enjoyed time with Bethany. He bought himself and Bethany a pair of Rollerblades and knee pads and the two of them skated all over our neighborhood community, stopping here and there to visit with our neighbors. Such a rare time this was—it was a *heaven-on-earth* time, joyful and peaceful.

Then, as the severance pay was coming to an end, Steve began to receive phone calls about job opportunities—one . . . two . . . three . . . four . . . and then number five was a phone call from a business friend in Tulsa who personally called Steve to say that he was retiring and to ask if Steve would be interested in interviewing for his position. Steve had turned down the first three offers and he was considering the fourth job offer in Las Colinas, near Dallas. He decided to accept the fifth offer for an interview, was offered the job, and he accepted it. Amazing timing, amazing God!

While Steve waited on the Lord's directive, he was given six months of severance pay, which we chose to use to refresh ourselves from the past year-and-a-half of transitional stress. We wanted to have fun and enjoy our family and friends in a leisurely fashion, but that is a Camelot expectation, don't you think? I don't recall that we ever made a conscious decision in our marriage to really, truly trust the Lord, but we do trust Him, as hard as it is at times when things don't go right or it feels like life isn't giving us a break. We certainly falter a lot in our trust, and we often want to take hold of the reigns of our future, but God doesn't falter for even a nanosecond.

During this time of career adjustment and transition, God dealt with some unresolved issues in our lives, namely my fear of no provision, my dislike for anything that might feel like discomfort, and my attitudes of materialism and greed. Did I like being confronted by these issues in myself? No, I did not.

It was the night before Easter when I had grown wary of the lurking unknown and began telling the Lord, "Okay, God, enough is enough of this 'sabbaticaling.' Steve needs a job! We are running out of money, God . . . " I was now beginning to be angry, and fear was more my friend than foe.

I went to bed that night thinking about Easter and what it must have been like for Mary, the mother of Jesus, and the other women who had been following Jesus. Were they afraid and uncertain about the security of their future? I went to sleep thinking about the uncertainty of tomorrow. Remember, this was the night that I encountered the scorpion in my closet.

"Jesus loves me. The Bible tells me so." He will go to great lengths to get our attention to tell us that He loves us and He will not forsake us—no matter what! At times, I still am tempted to give in to fear, but then I remember my testimony and the Lord's words to me, "The Lord has not given me a spirit of fear!" *I have to be conscious and radical in my thinking.* I refuse to let the spirit of fear land on me or poison my thinking. It is a decision and a battle, for *fear relentlessly opposes faith.*

Steve could have felt threatened or discouraged to be a fifty-three-year-old man without a job or plans for the future, particularly plans to be able to fund the girls' college educations and Bethany's future schooling (outside of Starbucks), not to mention future weddings. Instead, he received a whole new life message from the biblical account of Joshua and Caleb. This was the time to exercise our faith in the fact that we were entering a productive and fruitful period of our lives. God was instilling in us an attitude of adventure and faith, a willingness to trust God and take the risks.

While living in Dallas, we became part of a wonderful church body. We were asked by the pastors to begin and lead a ministry for young adults. We accepted the offer, and in a few short months, we found our home again filled with young adults seeking God. Not only did we love them, but they also loved us and expressed both a need and appreciation for what we could give them. What could have been a time of worry and discouragement became a season of great joy and fruitfulness. The time we spent in Dallas was just over a year, but in that short time, we moved into new levels of faith and trust, made friends that we still visit and who visit us, and met young adults who are married with children of their own yet continue to stay in touch. When the appointed time of sabbatical ended, the Lord opened just the right door.

Steve became the administrator for a well-known clinic in Tulsa. During the months and years ahead, Jessica and Rebekah completed college and launched into their careers and marriages, and our "little joy" at home, Bethany, was growing up.

Words for Reflection

"For it is God who is at work in you, both to will and to work for His good pleasure" (Philippians 2:13 NASB).

Can you look back at your life and see how God has worked, and is continuing to work, to bring His "good pleasure" to your life, family, work, and ministry?

Do you remember any mysterious workings and transformations? These are your testimonies—a very powerful weapon against the lies of Satan.

25

Heart Connection

The heart is meant to be connected and to stay connected—the heart has no purpose if it is not connected to a source from which, and to which, life flows. Ultimately, our hearts are meant to be connected to our minds and bodies, to the hearts and lives of other people, and to the eternal loving heart of God.

That is what a heart is for.

That is what a living heart *does*.

A heartbeat is usually the first audible sign that new life has been conceived. That first heartbeat cannot be heard with the human ear, not even the mother's ear—it is heard first by medical personnel using ultrasound equipment. The lack of a heartbeat often means a loss of life.

I had sensed that Grace Ann's heart had stopped beating within me, mostly because there was no movement where there once had been movement. It was the horrible news from the medical personnel who only saw a flat line on the ultrasound screen that confirmed what I knew as a mother— there was no heartbeat.

The horrible sound of a heartbeat that has flat-lined on audible heart monitors in a hospital is one of the worst sounds that I have ever heard, especially when it was the flat-line tone related to the disconnection of life support for Andrew.

Even so, Andrew did not *die* because his heart stopped beating—he died after his brain "crashed," in the words of his attending physician. His heart was kept beating with the help of a machine, and it was only when the machine was disconnected that there was no more heartbeat.

On the early morning that we unhooked our son from life support and we watched and listened to the monitors as his heart slowly stopped beating, *I truly felt what it means to be brokenhearted.* I felt as if I, too, would die. How could my own heart continue to beat when his had stopped?

I felt the same overwhelming shock and sorrow when I learned of Bethany's death. I felt as if I could just slide down onto the floor and literally die there physically. *Then I heard God speak, "My ways are higher."* My only reply was, "I don't know how anything high can come out of this, but I trust you." It was then that I felt His ever-sustaining presence and His grace strangely lifting me up.

But grieving time is different for every single person—no one can put rules and regulations on the grieving process. This sacred time is the Lord's time. Although there were times of relief, I still had the feeling that I needed to pull myself up by my bootstraps. Suddenly, I heard the Lord speak in my heart, *"You settle for crumbs, while I have a banquet table for you."*

I heard His voice loud and clear. Again, I don't remember all of the particulars of the events around me, but the Lord was right in what He said. I didn't want to settle. "I don't want crumbs, Lord. I want everything you have for me on this earth. Everything! And I will not settle for less, when you have more that you desire to give."

How often do we go through trials and sorrows using our own strength and ways, when the Lord lovingly wants to provide everything we need? He has already prepared a table for us; however, we need to come and sit with Him as He nourishes our soul with His life and love and healing. Take off your boots and let Jesus wash your feet and your heart.

God's Heart Is Always Good

The heart of God is always a good heart. It does not beat erratically. It does not occasionally skip a beat. The flow of life and love from God's heart is, has always been, and will always be life giving and life sustaining. Knowing and trusting Him keep us connected to His good heart.

It is only because of the goodness of God's heart that I can think of my children who have died and the two still living as all having a good life with the Lord, now and forever. His heart *is* the banquet table. There is so much more that He has for us, yet we often settle for so little.

I have had incredible opportunities to connect His heart with others. I have witnessed creative miracles through my prayers for individuals and have listened to their prayers of thanksgiving that flowed from a new heart. I have had the privilege of speaking to hundreds of women at conferences and witnessing the bounty of His heart relentlessly being poured out.

I suppose that is the greatest analogy for what happens when we ask Jesus to give us a new heart—that patient woke up as a revived man with a new heart, just as we who have had a spiritual heart transplant do.

I was given an awesome opportunity to attend a heart transplant executed by my brother Chip. I stood one foot away from the patient's head. I witnessed firsthand a sick and dying heart being cut out, exposing a dark and empty cavity where it had once been. Then I watched as Chip put a new heart in place, meticulously connecting the arteries and veins from the body to the newly installed heart. *Then I saw the shock—the bolt of power—that surged through the heart, and then the heartbeat! I was undone by witnessing the miracle of new life that had just been given to this man! Amazing, amazing grace.*

I suppose that is the greatest analogy for what happens when we ask Jesus to give us a new heart—that patient woke up as a revived man with a new heart, just as we who have had a spiritual heart transplant do.

We Cannot Compare the Sorrows of Our Hearts

Who am I to say that your worst day is greater or lesser than my worst day? Who am I to say, "If I had your blessing, I would be better"? Or even to say, "I do not know how I could have survived your loss"? Steve and I have not experienced the pain and loss that accompanies divorce or losing one's spouse, and there are many other tragedies which others have come through that we cannot understand. *It is important that we never compare our sorrows.*

I readily admit that we have never lost everything we owned due to a tornado, but we have experienced a fire that destroyed a large portion of our home, including furnishings and some possessions. Even in the midst of all of the disruption and discomfort that came from being removed from our house for much of the year, the Lord showed us His grace and protection.

As I worked to finish this book, we were facing the possible loss of a business into which we had poured our lives, finances, and resources for fifteen years. Everything went the other way, and the business cycle brought us within days of financial failure, including the loss of our home and all of our savings. We did not know how to face the problems and pending loss, so I prepared myself to finish this book in the midst of an impossible trial.

We cried out to God through the nights when the world around us seemed to be sleeping peacefully. We prayed together and separately throughout the days. We asked close friends to intercede for us, and our daughters and sons-in-law prayed without ceasing. We captured and confessed every promise that we found in God's Word—His faithfulness, His promises, and His instructions. The verse in the Bible that caught my heart and adhered itself to my mind was "Stand still, and see the salvation of the Lord" (Exodus 14:13 KJV).

> *The Holy Spirit still speaks and reveals Himself in amazing ways through amazing grace and amazing people.*
>
>

I made up my mind! Both in spite of and through my private tears, I was going to stand still and let the command and promise of the Lord come forth into my mind, will, and emotions. I was going to trust God and His ways once more. But this is not easy to do—I had to constantly think about what I was thinking! I had to constantly reel in the multitude of thoughts that were carrying me from the peace of God and the truth that He would not forsake us. His ways are higher and His ways are redemptive—He is the Redeemer, but He redeems in His way and His time (although I usually have lots of ways and advice to offer Him).

An intercessor and friend who prayed for us shared our dire business situation with another in confidence. *Something* or *Someone* touched the heart of the other believer, and in a matter of days, this man and his wife heard the Spirit of the Lord tell them to meet our desperate financial needs. We do not know the couple, we do not know their names, and we have never met them, but God spoke to them about us! God wanted to meet our need through them!

In a week, the funds to pay off all of our debts were given to us . . . *not loaned or invested . . . but given.* They were the salvation that the Lord provided for us. A friend once said, "Judy, you and Steve have certainly had more than your fair share of sorrow." I nodded, smiled, and said, "But God has given us more than our fair share of joy when He gave us His only Son. He may not respond to my ways, thank heavens, because His ways are so much higher!" That sounds so religious, but really, it is so true. I need everything that He has for me, and He promised me early in my walk with Him that He is complete for all my needs because He is my need. *The Holy Spirit still speaks and reveals Himself in amazing ways through amazing grace and amazing people.*

Types of Heart Connections

I believe there are four major types of heart connections that God desires for each of us to have:

1. Stay Connected to the Holy Spirit. The Holy Spirit is the One who keeps us vitally connected, because He indwells us.

I remember a time when I was asking for more opportunities to pray for the sick. One evening, just days after I prayed this request, I went to Barnes & Noble. I approached the door at the same time as a mother and a child with leg braces and crutches. I had the thought, *"What if I prayed for the child and she was healed?"* But I didn't stop and pray.

After I had let them walk through the doorway and followed in after them, I heard a voice in me say, *"You'll never know."* My heart broke, and I went inside, laid my head down on a table, and cried—which was far more embarrassing than if I had simply prayed.

I promised the Lord that night that I would not be ashamed to pray for healing if He prompted me to or if I was asked to pray. I have since prayed for many people in public and in private. I have prayed for two people with serious debilitating back injuries. Both were healed, and in both cases I could hear and feel the backbone moving into proper alignment. I don't know who was more thrilled—the two for whom I prayed, or me. I have seen the Lord do many supernatural things—I did my part and took the risk, while God did His part and healed and received the glory, which is as it should be!

The Holy Spirit is our counselor, our empowerment, our spirit of truth. I talk with Him as I would a friend. He is natural, and yet, He is holy.

It is the Holy Spirit who can show you more effective ways to do your work, reveal to you wisdom greater than any child psychologist could ever tell you about how to help your children, lead you to do healthiest things for your family when it comes to what you eat and what you do for recreation, direct you into the right decisions that will bring the greatest benefit to your life, and so much more! Beyond all of that, He imparts true joy for everyday circumstances. He enriches every relationship and truly blesses your efforts for maximum productivity and success! The Holy Spirit is the director of your life, not your peer.

It is the Holy Spirit who can and will show you areas in your life where you need to be forgiven and where you need to forgive. Unforgiveness robs you of joy, haunts you, and has the power to establish bitter roots in your personality.

Don't let time, distance, or pride keep you from the power of forgiveness. It is just not worth it! If our family could forgive the girl who convinced Bethany to drive with her to Stillwater that night, then I suspect you can forgive. At the same time, we need to remember that it is only through the power of the Holy Spirit that we are enabled to forgive.

Make an ongoing decision that you will not miss or put off the opportunities that the Lord puts in your path. Make a decision that you will continuously look for what the Lord desires, and then do only what He asks.

2. Stay Connected to Other Believers. First, it is up to us to stay connected to the Lord and to others who know and love Him. There have been times where I was overwhelmed at the way God sent people to me and Steve to encourage and help us, like when He sent the man and his wife to set us financially free! You can never know what our earthly connections can do in the heavenly realms.

3. Stay Connected to *Life*. After Bethany's death, I had a number of people tell me that they believed God was preparing me to be a grief counselor. Can you imagine? I can't! I have no desire to be a grief counselor, although many times I have counseled those in grief. I want to have joy, laughter, and live without regret or sorrow, and I want to counsel to joy. I am thankful for those who are called to the mission of grief, but I am not called. Even though I have suffered great sorrow, I continue to choose to live in joy!

This is not an easy choice, but it eventually becomes a natural reality. "The joy of the Lord is my strength," and I need strength in this world of ours.

A dear friend once said about me, "After repentance, Judy just wants to have fun." That's a pretty good simplified description of me.

Now considering myself to be in the category of "older women," I know there is a calling for me to speak to women about life and staying connected to the *real life support* that only God can provide.

I have clarity about my message. I have words of God's wisdom that I want to share with women, particularly younger women, about the Lord's desire to have a "heart connection" with them, not just in eternity but here and now on earth.

On a number of occasions as I have been speaking—often about topics that are sometimes related to ministry gifts, to hearing the voice of God, and to spiritual encounters with the Holy Spirit—I suddenly become aware that some of the women in the audience do not have a personal connection with the Lord. They go to church and may even believe that they have a relationship with Jesus, but they have never invited Him into their life as Savior and received His forgiveness. Jesus is our only source of a lasting life connection.

4. Stay Connected to God's Highest Purposes. Jessica and Rebekah each have three children, and I see them facing the same challenges that many young modern women do—challenges in balancing time and commitments and increased demands related to their children's education, extracurricular activities, and more. As I watch them and listen to them, I wonder, "Was I that overwhelmed?" Then, I begin to recall life before children—otherwise known as *B.C.*—where I participated twice a week in a friendly women's tennis league and had lunch with my friends, I was part of a Bible study group and taught a Bible study in my home, and I also did freelance commercial and residential design work. All of those luxuries began to fall by the wayside as children, one by one, entered the stage of my life.

I definitely had a schedule of mostly leisurely activities. Then I got pregnant, and soon enough, I couldn't play tennis anymore but assured the ladies that "as soon as I have this baby" I would be back on the courts. I still haven't gone back, and today, I don't even know where my racquet is.

Steve and I enrolled in natural childbirth classes, but then he forgot everything when it was time for me to deliver, and the doctor had to be my coach. Jessica arrived, to our sheer delight and thanksgiving. Then came Rebekah. Then came Andrew. Then came Bethany.

My life seemed to be reduced to serving Steve, my children, and other *needs* that arose. My plate was full, and most of the time, I felt overwhelmed with church activities, school activities, and social responsibilities. One day, I was pouring out my complaints to one of my older and much-wiser friends, saying, "I have to do this . . . I have to take care of . . . I need to . . . and . . . "

My friend stopped me mid-sentence and said, "Judy, you don't *have* to do anything. You *get* to. If you say 'have to' or 'need to' before a statement, then simply don't do it or stop doing it! If you don't believe something is a pleasure or privilege or rewarding, then you are overextended. Stop! If you take out your frustrations on your children or husband, then you are overextended. *You have settled for the good, instead of choosing the best."*

Wow. There I was, settling for crumbs. I stopped and decided I would start making choices based on the words that were coming out of my heart.

There is an ebb and flow to life, of course, but the continual crashing of waves and fighting against a constant undertow is not what the Lord has in mind for us. I was stressed to the max. I had to stop, repent, and change my thinking. My priority was to lead me to choose, intentionally and purposefully, what I believed were the best activities for myself and my family—activities for the whole family with interaction among parents and children. And then I had to let other things go, including the opinions of others and peer pressure.

There are two main things that I have come to realize about myself. First, I really don't care what other people think about me—perhaps that freedom is a benefit of having a prophetic gifting. Second, I did not have to contend with social media when I was a young mother. I believe all forms of social media should come with a label that says, *"Warning. This could be hazardous to your health and your family's health."* Repeatedly, I see extended use of social media stealing away a woman's time at work, at home, and with the Lord. Facebook posts, tweets, and photos on Instagram can stir up envy, jealousy, and insidious competition. I wonder with all of the *faces* that we see on social media, does the *face of God* ever show up in the posts and blogs? Sadly, social media is often a distraction from the reality of life. How many times do you hear a "ding" and half of the people in the room reach for their phones? Social media demands our attention more than the people we love who are sitting two feet away from us, across the table in a restaurant.

I carefully guard my need and desire for alone time to pray and listen. I certainly allow my alone time to be interrupted by the little people I know as grandchildren, my "Grands" as I call them, but I refuse to allow constant interruptions from a phone. Stop and think about what you value. One year from now or five years from now, will you even care about most of the messages you get in a day? Probably not. Chances are, you won't even remember them, and you might not even remember the people who sent them.

My Hope

My hope for you as a reader of this book is that you will desire a deeper heart connection with the Lord. I hope my testimony about the reality of life and the reality of the Lord's presence brings you to want more and to stop settling for crumbs. I hope that you will desire a real relationship with Jesus and increase in your knowledge of Him, getting to really know Him. I hope that you will experience His real-ness on this earth through the presence of the Holy Spirit within you.

> *I know that it sounds so religious, but the truth is, I would have despaired if I had not entered into the realness of a living God.*
>
>

I hope that you will become connected and stay connected to the true source of real life. Please don't let life, schedules, peer pressure, or anything else disconnect your heart from the only real and everlasting source of life. *I know that it sounds so religious, but the truth is, I would have despaired if I had not entered into the realness of a living God.*

Words for Reflection

"One generation *after another* will celebrate Your great works; they will pass on the story of Your powerful acts to their children. Your majesty and glorious splendor *have captivated me*" (Psalm 145:4–5 Voice).

What an awesome responsibility that we get to pass on the message of the Lord's glory and heart to the next generation!

May God grant us the desires of our heart that mirror His vast and awesome desires for us!

◇ **26** ◇

From Glory to Glory

I never wanted to be a participant in tragedy or hard times, but then again, who does? I have learned about life on this earth in the most painful ways, both from personal experience and from watching others struggle with very difficult situations. Every person will experience sorrow—it is simply part of the human condition and of life in a broken world.

The greater truth to remember in any time that might be called a "tragedy" is that God has made it possible for a human being to go through a fiery trial without being burned, and without even the lingering smell of smoke on their clothes. That possibility is His unending grace. The Bible promises to all who follow Jesus, "My grace is sufficient for *all* of your needs." Grace sounds so nice and pleasant, but in truth, it is fierce and relentless on our behalf.

It's like the story from the Bible of Shadrach, Meshach, and Abednego, who were thrown into the incredibly hot furnace of King Nebuchadnezzar. They should have died the second that they were tossed into the intense flames, which had been heated seven times hotter than normal, yet they emerged totally unscathed, with the ropes that bound them being the only thing that burned. What made the difference for them? The Bible tells us that a "fourth man"

> *Grace sounds so nice and pleasant, but in truth, it is fierce and relentless on our behalf.*

appeared in the furnace with them—His presence made all the difference (see Daniel 3:8–29).

Who was this fourth man? It was God Himself, in the very midst of the fire *with* them.

We, too, can be spared harm and emerge *alive and without even the smell of smoke*. It's amazing, and true!

Trust God—He Is Large and in Charge

A dear friend taught me the phrase "Trust God. He is large and in charge." How true it is!

Perhaps the greatest lesson I have learned in facing any trial is that we do not control the outcome, but we can control how we think as we go through it, and what we are willing to choose to learn from it. Again, it is our will that chooses. *God will never cross our will*—it is one of our greatest weapons against defeat, despair, and bitterness.

I have heard about glorious salvations coming from tragedy, about great healing arising from devastating illnesses, about reconciliations from seemingly impossible divorce stories, and about restoration after incredible brokenness. I rejoice in those stories, even as I realize that not all stories of tragedy have a complete reversal or even a genuine silver lining. Even so, the Bible tells us that God's ways are higher than our ways.

The bottom line that I know about sorrow is that joy comes in the morning. God's morning is not based on a twenty-four-hour clock—it is based on His timetable, with a guarantee that joy *will* come and will never be too late.

Anticipate the Coming Joy

Steve and I learned through the years that the joy that we eventually felt in the wake of our tragedies not only remained in our hearts, but also grew stronger and more complete through the years. There certainly are still times and seasons that we experience low ebbs that have lasted weeks and even months, but we will always recount our testimonies of God's faithfulness. When all is said and done, He has not nor will He ever forsake us. *Never!* Expect that to be true for you, too! Our testimony of His grace and love has not diminished. We have practiced running to our testimonies to find encouragement—they are our *safe place*.

True victory is the ability to remember without the tenderness of pain, and to voice thanksgiving without sorrow. Although I admit, when I see something or someone that reminds me of our chubby, smiling little Andrew or hear a song that our beautiful Bethany sang or played, I sometimes cry, but then I thank the Lord for His mighty redemption and powerful grace.

I have been asked at times if the comfort of the Holy Spirit can truly feel *real*. Don't ask me to explain *how*, but I *know* it is real and supernatural.

If we had not been able to put our sorrow and hardships on the mercy of the Lord, we would have remained bogged down in a state of grief and tragedy. In all likelihood, we would have developed layer upon layer of cynicism and bitterness, creating a hard shell of numbness around our hearts that would have kept us from becoming all, doing all, and experiencing all of the wonderful outpourings of God that He has given us and still has for us!

I would like to finish my story with John 21:23, which says, "It is from this exchange with Jesus that some thought this disciple [John] would not die. But Jesus never said that. He said, 'If I choose for him to remain till I return, what difference will this make to you?'" (Voice).

The moments of joy and blessing have been many, and we anticipate many more. In fact, we anticipate an eternity filled with them. The joy and the triumph are the Lord's, and we are in Him!

Words for Reflection

"But in all these things we overwhelmingly conquer through Him who loved us. For I am convinced that neither death, nor life, nor angels, nor principalities, nor things present, nor things to come, nor powers, nor height, nor depth, nor any other created thing, will be able to separate us from the love of God, which is in Christ Jesus our Lord" (Romans 8:37–39 NASB).

Notice that this verse refers to things "present" and "things to come." There is no mention of the past. God does not call us to live in our past or to allow things in our past to have power over us—we are to live now with a great awareness of God's overwhelming love and desire to help us at all times.

"They triumphed over him by the blood of the Lamb and by the word of their testimony" (Revelation 12:11 NIV).

So do we!

EPILOGUE

And Now . . .

What are Steve and I doing today? We are entering our retirement years, but we don't seem to be slowing down! We did go and follow our dreams. We are still parenting from time to time, but only when called on, and we are building our reputation as being the greatest grandparents to our six "Grands." We teach the younger couples' classes at our church and we continue to counsel, primarily young couples, from time to time. In all that we do and teach, our ultimate goal is to bring heaven to earth.

Life on earth is not heaven at all times. It takes overcoming disappointment and standing on the truth, and when all is said and done, God is good and full of grace and mercy. He will enable us in the end to overcome and come through to the other side. We can trust Him.

I have been speaking more often to women's groups and conferences. And, I have been urged to finish writing this book! It has been about a twenty-year process for me, and I can hardly describe how good it feels to reach the finish line. My family has referred lovingly (or not-so lovingly) to this writing as "*The Book*"—ominous for all who have endured!

The spurring to write came from the Holy Spirit and resonated deep within me because I have become increasingly concerned through the years that many of the young couples we counsel are not well grounded in the Word of God. They do not seem to have learned to recognize times when a written Word from the Bible morphs into God's spoken word through the Holy Spirit, often as a whisper in the heart. They do not seem to have learned to be still, nor have they trained their eyes to see the Lord in all His splendor, displayed in the changing of seasons, the majestic mountains, and breathtaking sunrises and sunsets. More importantly, they do not seem to have developed "the practice of the presence of God," which happens to be the title of a book by Brother Lawrence that I read in my twenties, and that I recommend everyone to read today. It seems to me that many can recognize the gentle ding of their phone better than the whispering voice of the Holy Spirit. But your phone, social media, and peers' opinions have no power to get you through when it gets tough.

It is out of these concerns that I have opened my heart and spilled my guts on these pages, not to instill fear or dread about life, but in an attempt to instill a deep desire to know God and to be known by Him—and to have an awareness that He truly knows, in detail, every aspect of His creation. He is my truest joy and I am His truest joy. He is peace when I think I can't make it, and He is the strength and courage I need to get me to the other side of the mountain in victory. As I heard an old man pray once, "He's my everything." And so He is!

There is a song I love, recorded by Darrell Evans, called "I Want to Know You." This song embodies the desire of my heart—to be so close to Jesus that I can truthfully say that I know Him and to be fully connected to His heart. How can a person fully know our infinite God? We cannot, although the Lord tells us that His desire is to forever reveal more and more of Himself and His heart to us. His desire to walk with us, talk with us, and express His love to us is far stronger than our desire for Him. What a lofty and glorious thing it is to know and be known by the Lord!

I have set my heart to know Him, to hear His voice, and to see heavenly visions while I am still on this earth. I long to learn and to do all that He desires for me to know and experience. I will not settle for crumbs when He offers a banquet table of His love, grace, and miracles.

I hope and pray that you will join me on the unfathomable adventure of faith that He promises to all who believe and follow Him! I have every confidence that the more you desire to know Him, the more He will reveal His unwavering love, His indescribable forgiveness, His undeserved mercy, His sustaining grace, and unimaginable miracles. You may even have the magnificent honor of hearing His voice, feeling His presence, or seeing Him in a dream or vision. No matter what, He will prove that He truly is love, joy, peace, and the giver of amazing gifts. What glory awaits us!

APPENDIX A

Tributes to Andrew

Throughout the years, various friends have told us what the experience of Andrew's death meant to them. It was not that Andrew *died*, but rather, it was the experience of how God Himself revealed His tender love and presence through the prayers and the fellowship of believers who gathered to comfort us and worship the Lord.

A Tribute by Bill Buergler

One of those who impacted us was Bill Buergler, who had served on the Mercy Medical Center Board of Directors with Steve. I feel certain that his first visit to the hospital was out of business etiquette and respect for his affiliation with Steve, but it was God who kept Bill coming back day after day. He told us later that the experience was the "purest thing" he had ever experienced. The presence of God—pure holiness—had touched Bill's heart.

Bill's triumphant response to this was an act of compassion expressed in the creation of a memorial to Andrew. It was a marble sculpture of a little boy holding a lamb. The inscription reads, "In memory of Stephen Andrew Swift—A little child shall lead them."

A Tribute by Kay Dishner

(As printed in the Fort Smith *Southwest Times Record* newspaper in September 1986, after Andrew's death)

The only way anyone can live and cope with the death of a child is by trusting God. We cannot give in to all of the "might have beens" but must concentrate on all of the things that were and are true.

The feeling of things being out of order when a child dies never changes, regardless of the age of the child or parent. A ninety-year-old mother who experiences the death of a seventy-year-old son would still be tempted to say, "Why couldn't he have had more time—why am I still here and he is not?"

For Mary, the mother of Jesus, it must have seemed disastrous when Jesus was killed at only age thirty-three. Her mind must have rebelled at His life being taken only three years into the ministry He had been born to do. She must have said, "Such a brilliant, healthy, handsome, sold-out-to-God man and here He is hanging on a cross in shame and disgrace! What a waste! Think of all He could have accomplished for the world and for Your Kingdom. God, if only You had let Him live! God, You could have stopped this. Why didn't You? God, how could anything good come out of such a horrible waste?"

Then, Mary saw as in a mirror darkly; now, face-to-face. Then, she did not understand. Now, she rejoices with all the angels in heaven every time another is born into the Kingdom of God because it was all made possible by the death of her Son! There was a reason. There was a purpose. It all did work together for good!

Her Son is the Way, the Truth, and the Life. Who but God could ever have known that this was the only way? Who but God could have accomplished such a magnificent purpose beyond all human understanding? Who, but God!

And so, Lord, we bow before You, gratefully submit to You, void of understanding anything but this: You are God. You are ABLE. You are WORTHY. We are Yours!

We are called by You, God, not to prove that You answer prayers but to be living monuments of your grace and glory! Lord, we strain to discover Your purpose. Let us strive to BE Your purpose.

Tributes to Bethany

A Tribute by David Bendett
(Senior pastor at Rock City Church in Corpus Christi, Texas and Bethany's former youth pastor)

Bethany Joy Swift truly lived up to her name in every way! Not only was she incredibly full of joy and life within herself, she had an infectious way of giving that blessing away to everyone she encountered.

Bethany was the embodiment of what all of us long to see from the generations coming up the ranks. She demonstrated her wondrous love for Jesus through her servant's heart and her worship. She was a singer, song-

writer, psalmist, and worship leader in our church's youth group. She was a poet, servant, prophet, evangelist, and artist. And to so many she was considered a best friend, one that was safe to cry with and patient to listen to those who felt desperate.

Such dichotomy between intense worshipper and childlike faith. She also was one of the silliest young girls I had ever met! From constant practical jokes in youth group that drove me crazy, to superfun dance parties, Bethany knew how to have fun and live life to the fullest.

Reflecting on Bethany's life is like a dream. My earthly dream and hope is that I can be a part of raising up a generation of mighty worshippers like her—full of life, wonder, joy, passion and purity for the Lord.

And so, I made the commitment to honor Bethany by carrying the bright torch of her life and legacy forward to the generations coming up behind me. Not only to my own children, but to the congregation that God has given me to pastor and impact daily.

I loved Bethany so dearly, and she will always hold a very special place in my heart. It is my desire as a pastor to do my part by keeping her memory alive within my heart by inspiring the next generation to be fun loving, Jesus loving, and sold out to Christ every day and everywhere.

A Tribute by Jessica Rice

(Bethany's oldest sister)

I remember Bethany Joy's debut on earth as if it were yesterday. She was truly a kiss of joy after the great sorrow of losing my brother Andrew, and my whole family celebrated and loved her with an attentiveness and appreciation for life and the preciousness of it. I was twelve years old, so for the beginning part of her life, I felt like a second mother. I would take shifts in the night to relieve my parents because she was not a good sleeper. I would watch her sleep and sing to her with a heart of gratitude. The difference in our ages, I believe, contributed to Beth's maturity as she was truly an "old soul" who had no problem "hanging" with the adults and grasping mature humor as well as deeper spiritual things in the Lord. She loved to laugh; she loved to be mischievous, she desperately attempted to use large vocabulary words (but mostly out of context), she felt things deeply and she was a good leader having no problems standing alone for what she believed. I would probably describe her as a social introvert. Her heart embraced people and time with them, but then there was that side of her that liked to pull back in and be at home.

As she grew up, there came a time in our relationship where a shift had to take place. No longer could I "second-parent" her. It took a little navigation, but we were beginning to function more like friends. I would have liked to have more of this. Beth held a sincere love for God. After she went to be with the Lord, someone gave us a copy of her singing a song at a twenty-four-hour prayer night where she volunteered to take the quieter and unseen hours of three or four a.m. She had come home from college for a weekend to be a part of this, one month before she passed. Her song/prayer to Jesus rang out, " . . . I have waited so long to see Your glory, To see your Holy of Holies . . . to see your throne room, to see the colors of Your throne room . . . Take me to the Holy of Holies, and never let me leave again." One month later she was there.

There are moments where I am in this place of worship or prayer, I feel a unity with heaven. And in that place, there have been times where I unexpectedly sense a closeness to her. There is not a doubt in my being that I will see her again. Through experiencing death on earth, there is a pull towards heaven that I have grown to love. The Bible talks about the Eternal intercessors and clouds of witnesses. I know Bethany is a part of that group in praying heaven to earth. Even in eternity her prayers move mountains, her worship turns the heart of the Father and her destiny lives on. "Your kingdom come, Your will be done, on earth as it is in heaven!" (Matthew 6:10).

A Tribute by Rebekah Sullivant
(Bethany's older sister)

My sweet sister, Bethany, is now one of the great worshippers of heaven. She left this earth November 12, 2006, and continued on to her destiny and life of worship in eternity with Jesus. We do not speak of Bethany in the past (at least I do not) because I do not believe she is "past"— I know with every fiber of my being that Bethany is only present. She now dwells in a place where there is no past and there is no future. She is more fully alive than I am at this very moment. That in itself brings such comfort and hope to my life here on this earth without her. However, when I was asked to write a "tribute" to her for my mom's book, I was conflicted with having to speak about her in the past. I would be forced to remember her as she was here, because the truth is, I do not know what my beautiful sister's heavenly life looks like. I can only long for that day. "Remembering" her or speaking about her in the past was difficult for me, because I truly choose to focus on her life presently with the Lord.

I wanted to take a few moments to honor her in every way possible—to honor the things people knew about Bethany, and the things they did not maybe know about her.

First and foremost, I want to honor Bethany's heart for Jesus and heart for others. She worshipped, she prayed, she wrote (oddly enough, she journaled a lot about heaven), and she ministered the love of the Lord to those around her. She longed for the things of eternity, she longed for heaven and earth to collide—mostly through the form of worship. She ministered quite a bit with a 24-hour prayer and worship ministry. She would worship at two in the morning on her keyboard when maybe only one or two other people were in the prayer room with her. She worshipped just as passionately with no one in the room as she did with hundreds in the room.

When it came to people, she loved the unpopular just as much as she loved the popular. She saw hurting needs that no one else would typically see, and she would make every effort to meet those needs. She gathered people together. She built community. As much as she truly loved to be alone, she also loved to be with the people in her life that were a part of her heart. She was always, and I mean always, ready for an adventure. She loved, loved, loved to laugh. She loved her family with every fiber of her being. She was dramatically loyal. She was dramatically fearless. She loved her home with my parents. Her home was truly her haven. She retreated and found rest and peace in her home. I remember at her age, I was always looking for a way to leave and go be with people. Bethany looked for ways to stay home. She was at peace with herself, she was at peace in her bedroom with a good book and a cup of hot tea. She loved her home, loved her dog, and loved her life with my parents. I always admired her peace and joy in being alone.

She had a deep love and understanding for music that I honestly couldn't completely share with her. I have been a professional musician now for over twenty years, yet Bethany had a hunger and appreciation for the history of music that I couldn't fully relate to. I loved that about her. I cannot imagine the musicians and the musical history that she is being surrounded by in heaven.

Last of all, Bethany has a smile that lights up an entire room, and a laugh that can ignite a fire that spreads so fast the room will become filled with joy in just a moment. That is why she is Bethany Joy. I can definitely say that last thing about her in the "present tense," because I know that now her smile is even brighter, and her laugh is even greater, because it now comes from eternal joy. She smiles from seeing the face of Jesus, and she laughs with the joy of knowing what living in wholeness is truly about.

A Tribute by Tim Cameron
(Headmaster of Metro Christian Academy)

I have had occasion to observe many students in forty-plus years as an administrator in education. Kids tend to cluster around sports, band, clubs, activities, or other common interests for sanctuary. I have seen very few teens that possess the security of identity, the depth of character, and relationship with Christ that empowers them to pass through the teen years without succumbing to the reality of peer pressure. Bethany Swift is my most profound example of such a young person.

Bethany was a gifted musician. She was a woman of stunning beauty. She carried an infectious joy about her that made you smile. But neither her gifting nor her appearance defined Bethany. Being in her presence I was impressed that she seemed to be living to please only one, Jesus. She was a good student, but not overly concerned about grades. Her lack of concern about academics alarmed me, but she got that right; I got it wrong. She had deep-hearted friendships, but was very comfortable crossing boundaries of age, appearance, handicap, race, and social strata to relate to one single person and give them her full attention. She expressed her love for others effortlessly.

Bethany seemed to float above the minefield of adolescence, impervious to the dangers, disasters, or sidetracks that lurked. She was in her own world, one that was consumed with Jesus. I watched how other young people related to Bethany. She had their respect because they knew she was uncompromising. They were attracted to her passion for life and the Lord. There was a fragrance about Bethany's life that reminded you what the love of Christ must smell like (2 Corinthians 2:15–16).

If anything defined Bethany, it was worship. She was our worship leader at a private Christian academy where I was headmaster. Bethany was a marvelous worship leader. However, she did not perform or just lead worship, she worshipped and brought others into the experience she was having. Worshipping with Bethany was an encounter you would not forget because you were being ushered into the presence of Jesus.

APPENDIX B

Jessica and Rebekah Remember
(Andrew's Big Sisters)

Jessica's Story

(Written at age twenty-two, unedited; she was ten years old when Andrew died.)

Time stopped when I saw my little brother floating in our pool. I grabbed his cold little body out of the water and saw the face of death. As the older sister, my heart broke when I handed a lifeless Andrew to my mother, who stood horrified at the edge of the pool. As if it was yesterday, I could describe every little detail down to what I was wearing—and what Andrew was wearing. But, is it necessary? What is my tragedy in comparison to another person's? The vital point of every person's story is what happens after the tragedy. So, this is where I will begin—at the point where most people feel that life has ended.

A fog of dust hid the gravel driveway as my mother sped away with Andrew to meet the ambulance we had called. Rebekah and I stood alone in a puddle of water on our kitchen floor. Silence stifled the helpless moment as we pondered what to do.

The next few minutes we were on the phone. Our voices quivered as we called Dad's office and told him what had happened. He dropped the phone and rushed off to the hospital. Next, we called Craig and Dianna Smith, our best friends. Then again, we stood alone.

Mom finally called and told us to go into our bedroom and pray. She knew nothing. Our only hope was in God.

Obediently, I led Rebekah to our bedroom where we fell to our knees. I remember saying, "Oh, Lord, please help Andrew, and give us your peace."

Immediately, I looked up and saw what I can only describe as a green blanket drifting down and softly folding itself over us. It was the peace of God. There was no question or fear as to what it was because its effect was evident.

This was the first supernatural encounter I had ever experienced with God.

When I was younger, I adored God. He was my friend. I remember swinging and talking to him, or climbing trees to hide my letters to Jesus. I never had needed the Lord, however, until that day . . . and He was there, my faithful Friend.

Some of our friends picked up my sister and me later that evening to go to the hospital. As we drove my heart grew more and more despondent as I speculated what I might have done to avert such an accident. If only I had not been so selfish as to want to climb trees. If only I had not said how I sick I was of being his babysitter. If only . . .

The elevator at the hospital stopped at the third floor. The hallways and cafeteria were filled with a sea of people. Most of the faces were familiar. These were our family friends, their children, the men building our house, and many others. The sea parted as Bek, my nickname for my sister Rebekah, and I walked toward Andrew's room.

Tubes were all over Andrew's body, connecting him to machines that mechanically tried to preserve his life, but despite the effort, he lay there ashen and lifeless. What I saw beyond the body, tubes, and machines was sobering. Somehow I knew. I knew that Andrew had seen the face of Jesus, and he did not want to come back. It was not the Lord who told me—at least I don't think it was. It was just something that I sensed, and in a strange way, I understood. Tears filled my eyes as I came to this stark realization that Andrew probably was going to leave us.

The next week is a blur in my memory. I cannot give an account for each day. Worship music filled Andrew's room fourteen hours a day. Nurses seemed to want to be with him, and many others gathered outside his room continually. The strange thing to me was that they did not congregate out of any sense of obligation, but rather, out of desire. There was a hovering presence around Andrew's room that I had never experienced. It was the Spirit of God. And to this day, there are many of us who cannot clearly describe or explain how it felt. Who can describe the living and ardent God? Who can capture in words a mystical encounter that is so profound?

Near the end of the week in the hospital, the doctor came to visit us at our house. Bek and I were not invited into the meeting, but we were very aware of the nature of the conversation. In that meeting my parents were asked to decide whether to take Andrew off the machines that were keeping him alive. Several days earlier he had opened his eyes and had begun responding to our voices. It was heartening to see his brown eyes again, but even so, they were not the same as before. That haunting emptiness that I had seen the first night lingered in them. I ignored what I knew and grasped for hope that he might live and recover fully.

The dreaded day came, however, when it was evident that only the machines were keeping Andrew here on earth. My family gathered in his room to say good-bye. Dad left, then Mom, then Bek . . . but I stayed. I wanted to be there when they let him go. My Uncle Chuck, a doctor, sat in the corner with me on one knee, and Chase, my cousin, on the other. The attending doctor came back with the nurse. I watched death gradually claim Andrew's body, and I wept.

The incident that I am about to describe changed my life forever. When the rest of my family returned to the room, Dad gathered Andrew into his arms and cried. I had never seen my daddy cry. Through his sobs, he prayed, "Oh, God, we do not understand all of this, but we accept Your will and Your way. If You desire Andrew, then we give him to You." With that, he lifted Andrew above his head as a very visible act of giving him to the Lord. Dad had led us all into a place of submission and release.

We embraced the reality that the Lord's ways are often beyond what we can comprehend, but that does not give us any right to rebel against Him. We put our trust in a faithful God Who has since proven Himself time and time again.

The weeks that followed were times of healing. One day I collapsed on my bed and prayed, "Oh, Jesus I feel so guilty for saying that I hated Andrew and hated keeping him. I would give anything to be able to keep him again." Through a tear-soaked pillow I cried, "Please tell Andrew that I really do love him."

The strangest thing happened after I spoke those words. Immediately I fell into a deep dream that I was in the Ozark Mountains sitting in our van. The doors of the van were open as if I was about to get out. Then out of nowhere Andrew and Jesus arrived. I do not recall when they came because my focus was on my little brother holding Jesus' hand. I watched, breathless, as his chubby grip let go so he could move toward me. He still had a "waddle" to his run. I grasped him into my arms as I had in the past. His head relaxed onto my shoulder as I said, "Oh, Andrew, I love you. I love you so much." He pulled away and I looked into his eyes. They were full of life and joy. Tears of joy and relief rolled down my cheeks as I watched him return to Jesus. And they left.

Instantly I awoke. That deep pain of guilt that I had carried was gone. Once again, my faithful Friend had heard my cry and healed me.

Twelve years later, a prophetic word was given to my parents that the Lord would complete the healing concerning the loss of Andrew. Little did they realize that this prophet was proclaiming my healing that would come shortly thereafter. I learned through the years that healing often takes place in experiential "layers." And, it is important that no one stops short of the completed work.

I had already embraced three specific times of healing, one being the dream I just described above. God had resolved the issue of guilt in me, erased the vivid and dark memories of rescuing Andrew's body from the pool, and He filled my emptiness and grief with His abundant joy. The healing was complete in me, or so I had thought.

A few months after the prophetic word came in 1998, a call came for Mom and me to go to the hospital and pray for a woman who was about to give birth in a premature delivery. As we walked down the corridor and into her room, I suddenly found myself revisiting an old familiar fear of death and tragedy. We stopped and prayed, but my heart sank into the vivid memories and pain that came flooding back in a totally unexpected way. I slid down the wall of the corridor to the floor, devastated by a wave of deep grief that engulfed me.

That day, I did what I had sworn I would never do. I asked Mom to take me to Andrew's grave. She did.

I kneeled there staring at the grassy area and pondering death and eternity. I was no longer a child, and my reasoning and mental understanding were *demanding new answers. Did I really trust God? He was faithful after Andrew's death—I could never deny that. But, deep inside, I feared what He might take from me next. I could not grasp the goodness of God. I only understood his goodness or mercy as the "comfort after the tragedy" that He had allowed.*

That time at the cemetery forced me to confront the truth that I was still not fully finished grieving.

A few months later, I moved to Dallas for a summer design internship program. I lived with a wonderful family whose home was filled constantly with the Lord's presence and people who loved Him. I had reached a precipice in my relationship with the Lord. I felt as if my love for Him was restrained in some way by my underlying fears. I lived for a week with tears streaming down my face. I cried at work, I cried with my host family the Wallaces, and I cried alone in my room at night. That week I surrendered to a God Who drew near to me once more, and there, He assured me of His goodness and the completion of this work of healing He had begun.

Later that summer, Bek and I stayed up into the early morning hours one night sharing with each other our memories about the day Andrew fell into the pool. We were both amazed at how we remembered the same details. In that conversation, I discovered that she, too, had entered into a deeper level of healing that very year. The prophetic word spoken over our family was fulfilled.

Andrew's short life helped shape my "knowing of God." Through his death, I found a God who met me as a ten-year-old and saved me from a life-shattering trauma. God met me at a place where no parent, friend, or psychologist would have. He came to me because He knew my thoughts, my fears, my pain, and even my confusion. He was just there. He listened to me. He drew near to me as I cried. He spoke to me. He comforted me, and sometimes, He was just silently present. He was truly my faithful Friend, who healed me and kept me from devastation. I found that the awesome God of power is also the most intimate and abiding Friend I can ever know.

Rebekah's Story

(Written at age nineteen, unedited; she was seven years old when Andrew died.)

As a musician, I am more comfortable singing than writing, but this testimony of the life and death of my little brother, Andrew, elicits so much emotion that I feel as if I am expressing myself in song. I hope you can hear this song—that there is a God who can and will bring comfort, hope, and restoration to you if you have lost someone who was a special part of your life.

In the midst of the comfort, you can come into relationship with the One who restores with joy. I have witnessed this restoration of joy, hope, and comfort in my life since the death of my brother, but only because I allowed the Lord to restore what had been shattered.

To share my part of the story, I want to begin with where I am now instead of taking you back to the day when Andrew fell into the pool. I was seven years old when that happened. As I write today, I am nineteen.

In 1998, I finished a nine-month program of discipleship training in Kansas City. The "Master's Commission" was an intense year of confrontation and change for me. God came to me in such a powerful way as He uncovered hidden hindrances and revealed new opportunities of life in His Spirit. I experienced great excitement for the present, vision for the future, and forgiveness and healing for the past.

Some of the most intense times for me involved reflecting on my past. Please understand that I consider myself to have had a wonderful past. I would want to change nothing in it. My family is a gift from God. The things I have learned from my parents are as priceless as jewels. But in April of my discipleship year, the class leaders assigned us to write about a "threshold" that we had clearly crossed in our past. We were to return to that threshold and describe our emotions at the time of crossing it, and discuss how the experience had changed us. As I began to recount my childhood, I remembered with fondness my years junior high and high school. I remembered growing up as a "pastor's daughter." There were many positive events and many challenges in that, but it was not within these memories that I found my threshold. None of the experiences of those years stood out.

I had thought initially about writing of the death of my baby brother, Andrew, as my threshold experience. But each time I started down that path, I felt a sharp pain in a very tender wound, and I decided I wanted to stay far away from exploring the depths of that tragic experience. After a few days of trying to avoid that threshold possibility, God kept bringing it back before me and I knew He was calling me to return to that experience I had attempted to bury long ago. I reluctantly began pouring out my memories in my journal, and before long, my emotions began to pour out of me like a river that had been dammed up for a long time. Perhaps the best way I can share this with you is to let you read a little of what I wrote in my journal.

Sunday, April 26, 1998

When I was seven, I crossed a threshold in my life. I know that I didn't realize it at the time. Now I clearly see how I entered that experience that day, and how I left it.

It was a gorgeous fall day in September. Perfect. Everything was perfect. My older sister, Jess, and I had decided that today would be the day that we would conquer the great tree in the pasture that we had not yet been able to climb. Without a care in the world, we ran across the field and began to scope out a way to achieve what had been up to that day an impossible task. Standing there, barefoot in the tall grass, we were faced with the fear of being bit by a snake. So, we decided to go back to our playroom where we had left our shoes. We raced through the field to our backyard, past the swimming pool, and up the stairs to the playroom. After finding our shoes in the mess of dress-up clothes from the party we had been at in our home a couple hours earlier, we headed out again to the great tree. We had no idea as we raced down the stairs that our lives were about to be changed forever. By the time we reached the bottom of the stairs, our innocent goals for the afternoon would vanish. Our adventurous mind-set would evaporate. Our carefree day would no longer exist.

Before we reached the last step, we looked out the windows and saw the body of our eighteen-month-old baby brother, Andrew, floating in the shallow end of the swimming pool.

I will never forget the feeling as I saw this picture before me. Everything stood still. The pain of that moment—part fear, part terror, part shock, bewilderment, confusion, and grief. It really was impossible for a seven-year-old girl to hold so many feelings bombarding her mind and heart in a matter of seconds.

I had raced up the stairs a carefree child. I came down the stairs a girl who promised herself that she would never allow herself to feel the emotions of that moment again. I didn't share that promise I made to myself with anyone. I'm not even sure I knew on that day how deeply that promise had taken root in my heart. I only knew that I was suddenly a different girl, and I didn't understand how that had happened, or why.

After Jess pulled Andrew's body from the water and handed him to Mom, Mom rushed off to the hospital and told us to pray. I ran into our backyard and fell on my knees. As loud as I could, I screamed in desperation, "Take me, not Andrew. Take me instead!" I think every person in our family probably prayed that brief prayer at one time in the week that followed. Looking back, I am amazed that I even prayed such a prayer. It was all I could say.

I wondered what God was thinking and feeling. His pain was surely greater than mine. Not only had He witnessed the death of His little boy, but also the death that was taking place in the hearts of each of us in the family that day. In me, I believe God saw a scared little girl who suddenly had a pain too big for her heart to bear. He saw her bury that pain deep inside her. He saw her confusion, anger, and disappointment in God Himself. And yet, I know God's heart only swelled larger with compassion and comfort for me in seeing my pain and sorrow.

After I finished that statement above, through many tears, I felt myself taken by the Lord through a deep healing experience. I mourned my brother's death for the first time.

When I later told my mom about what I had felt and had gone through, she responded, "Rebekah, you are allowing yourself to experience the healing that your Dad and I received years ago."

Jesus came with His grace and comfort in such a powerful way during the next two weeks after I wrote about my threshold. I could feel the inner healing taking place in my heart. I felt the anger and disappointment that had rooted itself in me being replaced with joy and peace. All of those years I had walked in a way that I had thought was bold and faith-filled, but suddenly I realized that I had closed down some of the deepest emotions of my heart. What a relief it was to allow the Lord to come and heal the wound inside me, a wound I had tried to bandage and forget, but had never been successful in healing.

How long can we bandage our own wounds? Some people apparently do this for a lifetime. But the bandaging is never entirely successful. Future disappointments and pain only pull off the bandages.

Psalm 147:3 says, "He heals the brokenhearted and binds up their wounds." That's what I experienced during those weeks in 1998. I witnessed the healing of my own broken heart.

I later shared this experience with my sister, Jessica, and discovered that the Lord had taken her through a similar time of deep healing at the *exact time* He had taken me through it. How faithful God is!

I urge you, if you have been deeply wounded by the loss of someone you love and cherish, allow the Lord to come and bind up your wounds. Invite Him to do the healing work only He can do. He is waiting and longing to restore something that has been damaged deep within you. He *will* free you from the pain you are holding if you will only allow Him to do it.

AUTHOR CONTACT

If you would like to contact Judy Swift, find out more information, purchase books, or request her to speak, please write to:

Judy Swift
contactjudyswift@gmail.com